Guiding Royalty

Guiding Royalty

My Adventure with Elizabeth Taylor and Richard Burton

by Yoram Ben-Ami
with Nat Segaloff

BearManor Media
2018

Guiding Royalty: My Adventure with Elizabeth Taylor and Richard Burton

© 2018 by Yodo Productions, LLC. All rights reserved. Except for brief passages in published reviews, no part of this book may be reproduced, converted, or transmitted in any form by any information storage and retrieval system without permission in writing from the author and with appropriate credit to the authors, source, and publisher.

Published by BearManor Media
and printed in the United States of America.

www.BearManorMedia.com

Library of Congress Cataloging-in-Publication Data (TBA)
Ben-Ami, Yoram, 1943 -
    Guiding Royalty: My Adventure with Elizabeth Taylor and Richard Burton /

ISBN: 978-1-62933-396-0

Excerpts from non-authorial interviews, letters, and other material appear under a Fair Use Rights claim of U.S. Copyright Law, Title 17, U.S.C. with copyrights reserved by their respective rights holders. Many designations used by manufacturers to distinguish their products (such as Oscar®, Academy Award®, Tony®, etc.) are claimed as trademarks or service marks. Where those designations appear in this book and the publisher was aware of such a claim, the designations contain the symbols ®, SM, or ™ on their initial appearance. Any omission of these symbols is purely accidental and is not intended as an infringement.

"OSCAR®," "OSCARS®," "ACADEMY AWARD®," "ACADEMY AWARDS®," "OSCAR NIGHT®," "A.M.P.A.S.®" and the federally registered "Oscar" design mark are registered and copyrighted by the Academy of Motion Picture Arts and Sciences.

Because it is not possible to include all credits on this page, additional credits will be found on page 133, which should be considered an extension of this copyright page.

Disclaimer: This book is based on actual events and individuals, although some events have been modified, some people have been combined, and some conversations involve speculation for purposes of dramatic storytelling and to preserve privacy.

Edited by: Robben Barquist

Book and cover design by: John Teehan

With love to my wife, Ani

Author's Note

RICHARD BURTON'S PUBLISHED DIARIES (Chris Williams, ed., New Haven and London: Yale University Press, 2012) include this entry dated Tuesday the 29th of August, 1975: "Sunned. Had tea with producer [...] at D'Alleves. Very German. Have a feeling this film won't surface either. Has the same air as *Jackpot*. Takes place in Israel so I might see it at last."

Burton was wrong. August 29, 1975 was a Friday, not a Tuesday. Moreover, he had met the "very German" producer at least a month earlier. On August 29, Burton and Elizabeth Taylor were, in fact, in Israel making a whirlwind tour that set the whole country on its ear.

This book tells that untold story.

Introduction

WHEN I MET ELIZABETH TAYLOR and Richard Burton they were what are called "lobby attractions." That is, when they walk through a hotel lobby, everyone notices them, cheers, and asks for autographs, but then never buys tickets for their films. Consequently, no studio or producer would hire them. Famously married in March of 1964, they noticed a subsequent drop-off in press attention when they were divorced in June of 1974. Desperate for publicity that would restore them to the front pages, and from there back to super-stardom, in 1975 they agreed to make a small film in Israel. Not only that, they announced that they were going to get remarried while in the Holy Land.

Dieter Kraus (not his real name) and I did not know of this scheme when he asked me to produce the movie when we met in a Tel Aviv cafe in the spring of 1975. As things unfolded, we became giddy with the prospect of establishing our big-time movie careers on the coat-tails of world-class movie royalty like Taylor and Burton. How could we have known that Taylor and Burton planned on clinging to *our* coat-tails at the same time?

More to the point, what was I doing in the middle of all this?

To make some sense out of it, I need to talk about Otto Preminger. Not many people these days remember Otto Preminger, but I must. He jump-started my career in motion pictures. He was a director, producer, and sometimes-actor who had a keen eye for publicity and a temperament that could be measured on the Richter scale. Among his screen successes—many of them controversial if not downright inflammatory—were *Laura* (1944), *The Moon is Blue* (1953), *Carmen Jones* (1954), *The Man With the Golden Arm* (1955), *Anatomy of a Murder* (1959), *Porgy and Bess* (1959), *Exodus* (1960), and *Advise and Consent* (1962). His personal victories included helping to break the Hollywood Blacklist by hiring blacklisted screenwriter Dalton Trumbo to adapt Leon Uris's novel, *Exodus*. He was an art collector, a wine connoisseur, a political activist, and an absolute tyrant on a movie set. And a movie set was where I worked for him.

In 1974 I was an up-and-coming (or so I hoped) producer in the Israeli film and television industry. I had done my share of television shows and small Israeli features and was living in Tel Aviv with my wife, Ani, whom I had met on one of those productions. She and I wanted to start a family, but to do that I needed to either move up in the film business or find another profession. Never lacking for chutzpah, when I read that Otto Preminger was coming to Israel to shoot a thriller called *Rosebud*,[1] I decided to pitch myself to him to become the Israeli production manager.

I happened to be in London staying at a friend's flat while looking for work when I obtained the name and telephone number of Otto's Associate Producer, Graham Cottle. He was in Cannes scouting locations with Preminger on before traveling to Israel to do the same. He was vague about giving me a job interview but promised to call me when the *Rosebud* company got to Israel in July. Naturally, come July, he didn't call, so one morning at 7 A.M., I showed up at the Hotel Dan in Tel Aviv where Preminger was staying and phoned up to Cottle's room asking to meet the Great Man.

I did this with a certain level of apprehension. I had already been warned by one of his departing crew members that Preminger was known for firing people (indeed, twenty of them would be sacked before *Rosebud* wrapped), but I forged ahead with the confidence and arrogance of youth; I was thirty at the time. Cottle answered and immediately became defensive; I sensed that he was put off by my aggressiveness. He told me that the job of Israeli production manager had already been filled, so I shifted gears and asked him if I could meet Preminger anyway to thank him for making *Exodus*. Cottle relented and told me to meet him at the Presidential Suite.

Preminger opened the door himself and stood clad in a dressing gown and slippers. The seventy-year-old filmmaker, with his gleaming bald head and blue eyes, looked at me like an elephant about to flick away a nagging mosquito with the end of his trunk.

"What can I do for you, young man?" he thundered in his automatically threatening Austrian accent.

---

1. Based on Joan Hemingway's and Paul Bonnecarrère's 1974 novel, terrorists kidnap a private yacht and the five young daughters of its owner. A counter-terrorist is dispatched to lead a rescue team. The film starred Peter O'Toole (replacing Robert Mitchum), Richard Attenborough, Kim Cattrall, Cliff Gorman, and Isabelle Huppert.

"I wanted to work with you, sir, but I understand from Mr. Cottle that the job has already been filled, so I only want to shake the hand of the great director of *Exodus* on behalf of all the film industry workers in Israel who share my feelings."

I wasn't sure how long I could stroke his ego before he realized I was brown-nosing him but apparently he had a high tolerance for bullshit.

He interrupted me to say, "Your name?"

"Yoram Ben-Ami!" I emphasized the syllables like the Voice of Israel announcer in English.

He smiled at me. "Oh, your name is exactly like the name of the hero of *Exodus*." (He misremembered his own film; Paul Newman played Ari Ben-Canaan. Ben-Ami? Ben-Canaan? Close enough, I guess.)

"Yes sir!" I agreed, nursing his confusion.

"Do you know the work of a production manager?" he asked.

"Yes sir."

"And how much do you want?"

"Money is not important, Mr. Preminger," I lied. "The same amount you wanted to pay the production manager you were going to hire." I played it with the presumption that he was interested in having me replace the other man.

"Your words indicate courage, young man. It is now seven-thirty. At eleven I want to go with my crew to scout locations where I will shoot my movie. It is enough time for you to find me the biggest and most beautiful cave that you have in your country." He rolled up his robe and turned around without saying goodbye. That's it. I was thrown into the deep end. Cottle, standing next to me, tried to save face by advising me, as we walked down the hall to the elevator, "Don't be so happy. He fires at least one person a day. Any day that person might be you—or me."

I managed to find the location Preminger wanted, and a lot of others, and survived *Rosebud*, even becoming something of a protégé to "Otto the Terrible." He flew Ani and me to the film's world premiere, introduced me around, and put his imprimatur on me.

Unfortunately, *Rosebud* tanked and did no one's resume any good. By the spring of 1975, with the film barely a memory, I was getting desperate for work. Plus Ani was pregnant. It all made me ask myself what I was even doing in the film business in the first place.

I suppose every child yearns to fulfill his parents dreams, but my mother and father had my to-do list already written when I was born in Ness Ziona in 1943. My birth came five years before that of the State of

Israel and the land, then known as Palestine, was still governed by the British Mandate. Despite our having little or nothing to eat, my mother, Clara, sent me to study the violin. Every Jewish mother in Israel wants her son to be the next Jascha Heifetz. It was not strictly her idea; she noticed that the neighbor's boy, Mordechai Aloni, was studying it, and she encouraged me to do the same. It didn't work.

As for my father, a simple construction worker, he was a hard man to please and he took his frustrations out on me with a strap. My sister Netta, five years my junior, avoided his wrath, but I did not. With every blow he gave me with his belt, any admiration a son could have for his father slipped away. Instead, I found my heroes in the movies: Errol Flynn, John Wayne, Burt Lancaster, and Gregory Peck. The movies also helped me learn English by comparing the subtitles with the spoken dialogue. By the time I was thirteen I had a passable knowledge of English. I also knew that I wanted to make movies.

My father disagreed. "A man needs a real profession," he said, " not *Luftgeschäft*," (German for, literally, "the business of air"). "He should be a teacher or a truck driver, something with permanence, something with a frame." He didn't begin to change over to my point of view—though I'm not really sure if he ever really did—until I started working in Israeli television in the late 1960s and some friends from Ness Ziona told him that they saw my name on the credit list. He sniffed. When he saw my name himself, however, he started to come around—but still not all the way. Even later when I was producing pictures all around the world and sent him photographs of me with famous actors, he wasn't impressed. I even sent him a picture of me with Bill Clinton when Clinton was Governor of Arkansas—I was filming a movie there—and that didn't move him, either. Why do children always want to impress their parents even when we know it will do no good?

Unimaginative people always try to dissuade you from your fantasies. I was brainwashed with the usual refrain: What are you doing? You're from Israel, not Hollywood. You do not know English. Everyone in the industry is a graduate of universities. You have no chance. I laughed. I am reminded of the speech that Jack Nicholson gave in 1976 when he won his first Oscar® for *One Flew Over the Cuckoo's Nest*: "Last but not least [I want to thank] my agent who advised me about ten years ago that I had no business being an actor."

I am also reminded of the story of the bumblebee. According to the laws of aerodynamics, the bumblebee shouldn't be able to fly. But the bumblebee doesn't know this, so he flies. For the last forty-five years, I have been this bumblebee. It has given me a career, a filmography, and dozens of stories. Yet the one that always comes to mind first is my baptism afire with the two greatest stars in the world. The press and public called them "Liz and Dick" but when we worked together I respected them as Elizabeth Taylor and Richard Burton.

In the adventure that follows, I have had to change a few names, combine some characters, and tweak some incidents, not only to make them play better but also to protect the privacy of some of the people who were involved in this unusual—and, at times, scandalous—adventure. If I went wrong on some of the things that took place in private, I hope I wasn't far from the truth, based on my observation, later conversations, and a genuine feel I developed for the people involved. It was also many years ago. As my writer/friend Nat Segaloff says, this is a memoir, not a deposition.

If what follows happens to read like a movie, that's the idea; I am working on bringing this funny, intimate, and strange story to the screen because I am, after all, in the business of air.

– Yoram Ben-Ami,
Los Angeles, California

1

I AM SURE ELIZABETH TAYLOR did not recognize me when our eyes met on the red carpet at the 1992 Academy Awards. I had aged; she had not. She looked as beautiful as she had seventeen years earlier when we worked together. I was there as a guest; she was there as a legend, the most glamorous surviving member of a vanishing era. The era may have been gone, but Elizabeth Taylor was not. Only 59, she was there to present the Oscar® for Best Picture. She was also there to remind us that they don't make stars like her any more.

Today the Internet and social media invent their own stars, and they come and go. But at the tail-end of Hollywood's heyday there was one genuine star who embodied the aura and history of the studio system that created and nurtured her. The screen could not contain Taylor's stardom; as she grew there would be the tabloids, the supermarket scandal sheets, the newsreels, and the paparazzi. Because of them, she became the most public of public figures and, while she claimed to be annoyed at the attention, she also played to the crowd—especially when she was married (twice) to Richard Burton, one of his generation's greatest actors.

Burton is less well known today than Taylor, and that's a shame. A robust and talented performer, he was nominated for the coveted Oscar seven times and never won. (After losing in 1970 for *Anne of the Thousand Days*, a ceremony which he and Taylor attended together, he never went to another). Over time, he forsook the stage for the screen and lost his way among the headlines, the romances, the drink, and the dreck.

Yet he did manage to turn his life around and, when he did, his career rebounded. It isn't widely known how he accomplished this, but I happen to have some insight. This is the story of how he found his self respect and how both he and Taylor set the young nation of Israel on its ear. I can tell it because I was there and a lot of it was all my doing.

If I had known that Burton and Taylor were "box office poison," none of what follows would have happened. But I didn't, and so (with a few burnished details to make sure that the truth emerges from the facts) here is the story of how I became an international producer.

I suppose every story of redemption has to begin at rock bottom. This one, however, starts at the top, and we need to go back a little. From 1962 until I met them in 1975, Burton and Taylor were not only the most famous actors in the world, but the most famous couple, period. They were royalty. They had begun their romance during the production of *Cleopatra* in 1962 while he was married to Sybil Williams and she was married to Eddie Fisher, but by 1964 they had divorced their partners and married each other.

Christened "Liz and Dick" by the tabloid press, Taylor and Burton flaunted their fame while insisting that their privacy was being compromised. Fur coats (for both), a yacht, a home in Switzerland (to avoid UK taxes), chartered jets, and sightings at glamorous parties added to their international prestige. When Burton paid $1.05 million in 1969 for the Cartier diamond as a gift for Taylor, their celebrity was sealed. So, everyone figured, was their box office clout.

Nobody told this to the ticket-buying public, however. Although *Who's Afraid of Virginia Woolf?* was a hit for them in 1966, their other co-starring roles were commercial flops and near-flops: *The V.I.P.s* (1963), *The Sandpiper* (1965), *The Taming of the Shrew* (1967), *The Comedians* (1967), *Boom!* (1968), and more. Although they could draw audiences as individual stars, their team efforts made it clear to producers that the $1 million price tag to hire Taylor, and a somewhat smaller fee for Burton, equated to throwing away money.

This did not tarnish their fame and they continued to dominate gossip columns and supermarket check-out line literature. If Taylor caught a cold, it was front page news. If Burton eyed another woman, the tabloids said he was cheating. Perhaps for these, or any other number of reasons, Liz and Dick divorced in June of 1974.

With fame comes pressure. Taylor handled hers with humor, grace, and the training she had acquired as an MGM contract star. Burton— equally bright, gifted, and charismatic—handled his with a bottle. By October of 1974, four months after his publicized divorce from Taylor, he was starring as Winston Churchill in a BBC television movie called *The Gathering Storm*. Neither of us could know it yet, but this was his first step on a journey that would very soon bring him across my path thousands of miles away.

* * *

I was living in Tel-Aviv with my Israeli-born wife, Ani. We had been married in July of 1973 when I was producing Hebrew-language movies made in Israel and she was a script supervisor on one of my shoots. Now we were trying to start a family. I was also trying to advance my career.

In England, the people working with Richard Burton must have been wondering what happened to his career. At 49 years of age, Burton seemed older, even under the make-up that made him look like Winston Churchill, whom he was playing. The film was about Churchill, who, at 66, had been asked to assume the position of First Lord of the Admiralty by King George VI in May of 1940 when civilization—or at least the United Kingdom—stood perilously at the brink of what would be called World War II.

Churchill was up to the task. From what I heard and later pieced together, Burton wasn't. Summoned from his dressing room by a cautious Assistant Director, he stumbled across the soundstage, steadied himself on a wooden strut, and gathered his gumption before stepping onto a replica of Churchill's office.

Both Burton and the set were brightly lit. Director Herbert Wise, noticing this, signaled the Assistant Director for a clue. The A.D. tipped his cupped thumb and hand to his mouth to mime "he's been drinking." As the crew poised to roll tape, Wise approached his star.

"How are we feeling, Richard?"

Burton looked at him through watery blue eyes. "Churchillian."

Wise pretended to ignore the smell of vodka. Burton was renowned to be able to go through a large bottle in the course of a day. It was ten in the morning.

"We'll take it from you standing at the table," Wise said as if nothing was wrong.

"Would you mind if I sat down for this?" Burton said. "I think Churchill would be sitting down."

Wise knew that he had to keep control of the set. "He's just been made First Lord of the Admiralty after Hitler invades Poland," the director explained as evenly as he could. "His staff is waiting for him to say something. Don't you think he'd be standing?"

Burton answered the question by sitting heavily in his chair. "Carry on, then," Wise sighed. "Roll tape."

The crew tightened into a production unit and set everything in motion. "Action," Wise said crisply. An officer entered and saluted Burton/Churchill.

"Mr. Churchill, German radio is accusing you of planting a bomb and blaming it on them to inflame the British public." The actor paused for Churchill's scripted response.

Burton was silent. The camera remained on him.

"How many lost?" The response came not from Burton but from the Script Supervisor offscreen helping him to remember his line.

"How the hell should I know how many lost?" Burton said, addressing the Script Supervisor, not his fellow actor.

"That's your line, dear boy," Wise said. Burton said nothing. Wise continued, "Have we been misbehaving, Richard?"

"Just one or two little ones to loosen me up," he said, his voice starting to slur. "God knows I've done worse. God knows so did Churchill."

"Not before a take, he didn't."

Burton brightened with some far-off remembrance. "Did I ever tell you my Churchill story?"

Wise frowned. "For God's sake, Richard, not now."

Burton ignored him. "I was doing *Hamlet* at the Old Vic in '53," he began as Wise seethed, "and the director came backstage and said, 'do be good tonight because the Old Man's in the front row.' Of course, to anyone in England at the time, he meant Churchill. I went on and was into my first speech: 'Oh that this too, too solid flesh would melt, thaw, and resolve itself into a dew, or that the everlasting had not fix'd His cannon against self slaughter. . .' Immediately there was a dull rumble from the front row. It was Churchill, and he was speaking the lines with me. And I could not shake him off. I tried going fast. I tried going slow. I did cuts. Every time, he'd grumble and then catch up with me."

Ignoring Wise's growing pique, the crew was mesmerized with Burton's name-dropping recollection.

"Finally," the star continued, "during the interval, I was in my dressing room and suddenly the Old Man appears in my doorway. He says, 'My Lord Hamlet, may I use your lavatory?'"

The set was silent. The crew didn't know whether to laugh at the story or admonish the man who told it. As if to rescue everyone, the Assistant

Director said, "We're still rolling tape, sir."

"No we're not," Wise shot back. "Cut. That's a wrap."

"That's a wrap, everybody," the A.D. repeated, and crew members began dousing lights and stowing equipment for the day. Wise approached Burton like a teacher about to berate a naughty student.

"They said you could hold it together long enough for us to finish."

Burton raised his glance. "How far did I get?"

Wise shook his head. "You're finished."

Burton started to rise. "I'll be in my dressing room," he said, but he couldn't stand up. He sank back into his seat. Wise left him there.

His drinking was not helped by his next filmic adventure. In early 1975 he joined the troubled production of *Jackpot* after its original star, Robert Mitchum, pulled out over concerns about financing. Burton didn't need the money; he needed a movie, and agreed to join co-stars Charlotte Rampling and James Coburn under Terence Young's direction. The picture was never completed, not because of Burton but because its backers went dry, but it left the odor that Burton wasn't a big enough name to attract new backers, and the damage was done.

* * *

While Burton was hitting rock bottom in England, I was at the end of my rope in Israel. It was August of 1975 and I was getting desperate. The Israeli film industry was a tightly knit society; people either knew you and hired you or you knew people and hired them. Films had to be kept to a low budget because they had to earn back their cost at home; relatively few were sold outside the country because we made them in Hebrew, and very few people in the world speak Hebrew. For Ani and me, things were tight. God blessed us and she became pregnant, but He must have been busy after that because I still couldn't find work.

At this time, the Israeli film industry was largely local. Although western filmmakers like Otto Preminger (*Exodus*, *Rosebud*), Norman Jewison (*Jesus Christ Superstar*), and a few others had used the country for location work, most movies born and shot in Israel stayed in Israel. My ambitions were farther-reaching.

Thousands of miles to the north in Celigny, Switzerland, two other folks were looking for work, too, and they couldn't understand why there was none to be had, even though they were two of the most recognizable people in the world.

Elizabeth Taylor, wearing dark glasses and with her head wrapped in an expensive silk scarf, stepped into a medical clinic and waited for the attention of the young male clerk at the reception desk.

"I'd like to see Dr. Lesneski, please," she said in a low voice.

"Do you have an appointment?" the clerk asked, not looking up.

"He hasn't returned my calls and I need to see him," she said. Her voice was calm but insistent like someone who wasn't used to having her requests questioned. "I drove over in case he was in."

"I'm afraid you should have made an appointment," the clerk began, then raised his head at the moment Taylor removed her dark glasses. The color drained from the clerk's already pale Swiss skin. "I'm sorry, Miss Taylor, I'll—I'll tell him you're here." He tried lifting the telephone receiver but missed several times, his stare locked onto the 43-year-old Taylor's magnetic violet eyes.

Within three minutes, she was being accompanied by Dr. Lesneski down the carpeted hallway of the clinic toward the private—indeed, top secret—suite of its most famous patient, Richard Burton.

"He's responding well," Lesneski told Taylor. "He's really taking this seriously."

"I should hope so," Taylor said. "I think this time should do it." She sounded as though she was trying to convince herself of something with which she hoped the doctor would concur.

"But you need to be aware of some changes in his personality." He stopped a few steps from Burton's door.

"What do you mean?"

"A man who has consumed as much alcohol for as many years as Mr. Burton has, in a sense, rewired his brain. As a result, he may exhibit certain unusual behavior at various times, especially in moments of stress."

"What kind of behavior?"

"He'll recover eventually, but in the meantime he may have exaggerated reactions to some kinds of situations."

"Tell me what kind of behavior," Taylor insisted.

"There may be some extremes."

"That can't be any worse than it was before he checked in here," she said.

"He may be anxious, impatient, even intolerant at times."

"That isn't so different from the way he usually is."

"He might have been that way in the past because of his drinking. He may be that way now because he's not drinking."

"Then what the hell's the advantage of not drinking?"

Lesneski was hoping to make his point dramatically. He put his hand on Taylor's arm. "The difference is, Miss Taylor, that if he does not stop drinking, he will die."

She let it sink in. "I understand. What can I do to help him?"

"Let him depend upon you but don't let him know it."

"That may be awkward. We're no longer married. What am I supposed to do, stop by for coffee and forget to leave?"

"I'm sure you'll find a way," the doctor said. Taylor sighed and nodded as Lesneski knocked on Burton's door.

"Who is it?" his rich Welsh voice bellowed from inside.

"Mr. Burton," Taylor said, snapping into happy mode, "you have a guest."

Burton opened the door, greeted Taylor's smile with his, and they embraced. Lesneski immediately saw that his presence was no longer required, and he departed. Neither Taylor nor Burton noticed him go. They entered, still embraced, and shut the door to be together.

Before long, their conversation turned to their futures, or lack of them.

"I refuse to believe it," Burton said, pacing in reaction to Taylor's news.

"You must," Taylor insisted, searching the room for something. "We're the most famous unemployed stars in the world."

"What on earth are you looking for?"

"Isn't there anything to drink around here?"

"Good Lord, Elizabeth, this is a sanitorium, not a tavern."

"I meant a club soda or something."

Burton reached for a small, in-room refrigerator. "I can offer you mineral water." Taylor waved it away. Burton continued. "I do have some good news. My lawyer says there's a chance of a movie in Israel." He handed her a script bound in brown cardboard covers. She hefted it in her experienced hands.

"I'd say it's 125 pages," she said.

"Very good," Burton said. "120 to be exact."

Only then did she read the title. "What does *Vergeltung* mean?"

"It's German for 'retribution.'"

"I forgot you spoke German," she said. "It sounds like a mouth disease. It certainly weighs enough. Is it any good?"

Burton took it from her and laughingly flung it onto a nearby chair. "It's 120 pages of pure, blessed, unadulterated horseshit. This German chap, Dieter Kraus, wants to shoot it in Israel and says he can raise the money."

"I'm glad one of us is working," Taylor said. "How much do you get?"

"I took a slight salary cut," Burton answered evasively.

"Richard—?" Taylor taunted as if she were talking to a small child.

Burton dug his toe into the carpet exactly like the little boy Taylor's tone made him feel like. "Fifty thousand dollars."

"Fifty thousand dollars?" she asked with soft incredulity.

"And a few net points."

She shook her head in disbelief. How far had he fallen from the lush days when $750,000 would be rejected as insulting? Or her own asking price of one million? Finally she calmed down and asked, "Is that the best they can do?"

"No, my love" Burton responded weakly. "It's the best *I* can do." Then he added, "there will be more money when the picture rolls. The purpose of this visit is to draw attention to the project."

Elizabeth Taylor was no fool. Celebrated for her beauty, she was also possessed of a dry wit and sharp tongue that didn't contradict her appearance, it enhanced it. When she was an MGM contract actress everybody loved her; not only did she brighten a set, she coalesced it. The gift of observation that made her an Oscar-winning actress also made her a trusted, stalwart friend. It was she who was the first to arrive at the site of Montgomery Clift's tragic automobile accident on March 12, 1956 when the drunken, emotionally torn actor left her Beverly Hills home after a dinner party and piled into a telephone pole. It was she who bonded with Rock Hudson on *Giant* in 1956, a friendship that influenced her charity work concerning AIDS later in life. Now here she was, acting more like a mother than a wife to her former husband.

Although fiercely in love throughout their ten-year post-*Cleopatra* marriage, Burton and Taylor hit rough road over his drinking (not that she didn't drink too) and brooding Welsh temperament. Likewise, she could also be moody; years of being pampered led her to expect gifts and attention, something the working class, no-nonsense Burton found frivolous, yet still indulged. She was raised to be a princess; he raised himself to be a prince. The differences played against them, but, still, there was affection, which is why Taylor reacted to *Vergeltung* by saying, "Israel? How marvelous. When do we leave?"

Burton was stunned. "*We?*" he said. "*I'm* the one they're hiring, dear heart—for a pittance, let me remind you."

"I've never been to Israel," she pouted.

Burton tried logic. "It isn't a 'go' project yet. They're still setting it up. We won't be shooting for a couple of months. God knows I don't want to have another disaster like *Jackpot*. This time there'll be no acting until the money's in the bank."

"Maybe if we went there now it would light a fire," Taylor prompted. "We can help them raise the money—and help ourselves. When do they intend to start shooting?"

"Perhaps by the end of the year."

"We can't wait that long," Taylor said, a wisp of desperation edging into her voice. "While you've been in here, we haven't been on the cover of one magazine. Not one. Not even the local channel listings."

"And I suppose you've been standing in all the supermarket lines to make sure."

"It isn't funny, Richard," she admonished him. "Since our divorce all they write about is Tatum O'Neal. No, we need to take back the spotlight now."

"By the time I get out of this place, I'll be sober."

"By the time you get out, we'll be forgotten."

At this, Burton gave a hearty laugh and bowed to his ex-wife as if she were regent. "No one on earth will ever forget you, dear heart," he said comfortingly. "You can rest assured of that."

"Rest?" she said. "I'm only 39. I'm not ready to rest."

"You're 43, and I didn't mean retire. I meant you should have confidence. Don't be so prickly. Think of it this way. An actor works because he *has* to, but a star works because she *wants* to." He paused to make a point. "I've spoken with our accountant. He says each one of us has enough money never to have to work for the rest of our lives."

"Don't play word games with me, Richard," Taylor grumbled. "The fact is that I *want* to work. The truth is that no one wants me to. We need to make them want to hire both of us. Besides, it's no fun acting opposite anyone else. You keep me on my toes."

"And you keep stepping on mine. That's why we got divorced."

Taylor ignored his dry comment; she knew how to take one of Burton's verbal bullets. She was also mindful of the doctor's warning about his mood swings. Instead, she tossed her head back, which she did when she got an idea. Burton saw it and knew what it meant. Finally he said, "You're scheming something, aren't you?"

"Whatever makes you think that, dear heart?" she asked schemingly.

"Because I know you better than I know myself, and I see your gears turning."

"All right," she said. "Why don't you let these mouth disease people know that you'll be happy to come to Israel for advance publicity. Spend the fifty thousand now to raise the rest. Tell them you want to get a feel for the locations or something. You want to meet public officials. You know the drill."

"Really, now, Elizabeth, we can't just up and go there like some Hadassah group. This will need planning, security, a formal invitation from the government, advance work—"

"That's the idea!" she perked up. "An official visit will draw every reporter there is."

Burton paused. There was something missing.

"Every plan has to have a secondary purpose," he said, the drama teacher in him starting to kick in. "Just going there won't be enough to get publicity. We can drive to the airport in Zurich and get a two-column photo buried near the travel news."

"You sell us short," Taylor said, "People haven't seen us together so long that it's time to play the 'Liz and Dick' card."

Burton reacted thoughtfully. "It might work at that."

"Of course it will," she agreed, sitting beside him. "Plus, your lawyer settled on a lousy fifty thousand. The least he can do is pull a few strings and get us some perks. It ought to help that I'm Jewish."

"Yes, and something beside that," he said, his voice trailing off.

"Are you brooding or thinking?" Taylor prodded. "You're a Welshman and I can never tell." She waited for him to say something. "Well, what do you think?"

Burton made no response, He held up his hand to silence Taylor and took a pose, staring out the picture window at his magnificent view of Celigny's mountains and picturesque streets. The town was its own fairy tale. Why not invent one of his own?

"We need to create more of a buzz," he said, turning slowly and smiling seductively at his ex-wife. "I have just the idea." He moved slowly, cat-like toward her. "I've been contemplating it ever since we divorced." He waited dramatically, then said, "Elizabeth, my dear one, my queen of queens, would you marry me again?"

Taylor laughed disbelievingly. "What's in all that mineral water you've been drinking?"

"Call it truth serum. Call it ambrosia. I don't care what you call it, but I'm serious. We should get married again, and what's more, we shall do it in the Holy Land. Think of it!"

"Are you mad?" She recoiled. "The blood's still wet on our divorce papers."

Burton sidled closer to her. "It would make headlines all over the world, and we can both use the buzz."

"I was rather hoping you'd say it was because you're still in love with me."

"Oh, but I am," Burton said. "And I especially love your buzz." He got down on one knee and placed his hands over his heart. "Marry, so I mean, sweet Katherine, in thy bed. And therefore, setting all this chat aside, that you shall be my wife, your dowry 'greed on, and will you, nill you, I will marry you."

"That's from *The Taming of the Shrew*," Taylor recognized. "And they said I couldn't do Shakespeare! I mightn't, if you hadn't been with me. But I don't see how—"

"Now, Kate," Burton continued, reciting the Bard, "I am a husband for your turn, for by this light, whereby I see thy beauty, thy beauty that doth make me like thee well."

Taylor smiled and played along: "Oh, Petrucio!"

"Thou must be married to no man but me, for I am he born to tame you, Kate."

"We'll just see about that," Taylor said, breaking character. "It may have worked for Shakespeare but I'll be damned if I'll let you get away with it this time."

Burton dropped his acting façade and spoke to her honestly, as himself: "Elizabeth, I am indeed serious. Will you re-marry me?"

She flung herself into his arms and kissed him deeply. Such was her way of saying "Yes."

Looking back, this planning session was the only way to make sense out of their behavior in Israel, especially Burton's, who never found the time to discuss the picture he had come there to make. But that realization was to hit me when we were all in too deep to get out.

2

RUDIKA, MY ISRAELI AGENT, HAD given me the name of a German producer named Dieter Kraus who wanted to see me about a job. He had made a number of documentaries in Germany but, like all of us who were infatuated with movies, feature films is where he wanted to be. He had, she said, a script that he wanted me to take on but she was unclear what the financial arrangements would be. "I don't really know him very well or if he has money," she said. "Try to find out yourself." I agreed, saying, "What have I got to lose?"

I thought about that as I wound through messy Tel Aviv traffic on my way to a coffee shop where Dieter Kraus and I were to talk. I was alerted to look for an extremely well-dressed, tanned, blond-haired man of about forty-five. I was not concerned that I might fail to recognize him given the overwhelming number of dark-haired, dark-skinned men and women who made up Israel's population. What I found impressive is that he recognized me first.

"Yoram, over here!" he called from a small round table at the back of the cafe. "I am Doctor Dieter Kraus," he said, shaking my hand. "*Wie gehts*."

"Yoram Ben-Ami," I returned. "*Shalom*."

I immediately noticed that Dieter smoked underhanded, with his palm up, pinching the cigarette in the European style. That I had also seen this done by German officers in countless Hollywood films about World War II made a first impression I had to make a point to overcome.

"Your agent described you well," he began.

"She told me about you too," I said, "especially that—"

"You will sit?" he interrupted me. I know it was supposed to sound like a polite suggestion, but it came out sounding like an order.

"—you are German," I finished.

"Ya," he said. "Does that bother you, being a Jew?"

"Not at all," I said. "Somebody has to be German. Why not you?"

Dieter took it the right way and smiled. I smiled back. There might be hope.

"She also said that you have a script that you want to film here in Israel," I began.

His blue eyes widened. "Not just a script, Yoram, a *masterpiece!*"

"And you need an Israeli producer."

"Also correct," he said. "Coffee?"

Before I could answer, Dieter snapped his fingers at a waiter who just then was passing by. Yes, I said to myself, he is German, all right. I don't know what the waiter thought, but, from the look on his face, it wasn't "have a nice day."

Dieter launched into a pitch describing his masterpiece. I half-listened, choosing instead to make a visual analysis of the man who wanted me to work with him. He was dressed in what hung like an expensive summer suit; its shoulders didn't sag even when he slouched in his chair. The watch on his left wrist had a woven band and was not ostentatious, yet I could see it was worth a small fortune. His wedding ring was either platinum or white gold, quite discrete, and the collar of his Oxford shirt was crisp even in Tel Aviv's July weather. He wore a tie, something that would have made him stand out even if he hadn't spotted me first.

"I have the greatest script with the greatest story you have ever read," he continued pitching. "It is about a former fighter pilot who drinks himself out of a military career and the only job he can get is crop-dusting. He meets an American divorcée by the name of Katrina who is visiting Israel and the two of them become involved in a plot of murder, revenge, heroics, action, and, of course, romance."

I'd heard pitches like this a hundred times. Sooner or later they all sound the same. Every one of them is a sure-fire hit so great that, first, no studio will touch it or, second, the producer won't risk letting a studio see it for fear they'll steal it, and this is why we're going the independent route. What this really means is that the project stinks and nobody in the business will take him seriously. But you never know, so I kept listening—right up to where he said, "This will be the first movie that I shall direct and your first international movie that you will produce." Perhaps he saw a look of skepticism flash across my face, but he plowed ahead regardless.

"It is titled *Vergeltung*," Dieter said, "but the main thing is, it's a love story."

"Naturally," I said. Then something he told me earlier rose to the surface. "You said you're a doctor. A doctor of what? Dramatic writing, perhaps?"

"*Nein*," he said. "I am a dermatologist."

"Naturally," I repeated.

"What is the matter?" Dieter asked. "Do you not like dermatology?"

"This is a movie, not a pimple," I said, "and dermatology is not directing."

"Do not worry. I have directed documentaries. The dermatology is what gives me the name 'Doctor.' Some people are impressed more than you are."

"Naturally," I repeated.

"You do not like my idea for a film?" Dieter pressed. "You do not believe in love perhaps?"

"I believe in love," I said. "What I do not believe in is bullshit."

"Bullshit?"

"*Schwachsinn*," I said. I may not speak much German but, growing up, I managed to stockpile a few curse words. "Where's the money?"

"Ach, the money," he said as though the very thought was vulgar. "I budget this film at between four and five million American dollars."

"How much money have you raised so far?"

"I will be honest with you," Dieter started. "I am not drawing a salary at the moment. I am putting all I have into the film. If you agree to produce, I will ask you to do the same."

I was gobsmacked. I'd known him for five minutes and he was asking me to work on spec—for free—on a project I hadn't even read yet. I told him no.

"It will only be until we start shooting," he assured.

"That could still be months away. What will support my wife and me through breaking down the script, budgeting, scheduling, casting, and getting location permits?"

"I'm sorry," he said, "but I'm taking—how do you say it—a hit on this, too." He wasn't helping matters.

"How much money do you actually have in the bank?" I asked.

"Fifty thousand American dollars."

"Is that seed money?"

"I do not understand."

I swallowed hard. For a man who said he had produced even documentaries, I wondered how much he actually knew about making feature films. "Seed money is the money you spend to raise the rest of the money. It's money you use to get started with. Planting a seed, get it?"

"Oh," Dieter said. "There will be more money coming. It will be here."

I stood up and said, "I'm sorry, I've got to go."

Dieter couldn't believe that I had left him in the middle of a conference. He softened and said, "Wait, wait! Please sit down. I am not asking you to raise the money; I am asking you to spend it. Please sit. I will show you what will bring in the money."

Our coffees arrived and the waiter placed them on the table while Dieter fumbled with his leather case. I thought the waiter placed Dieter's cup dangerously close to where it could easily tumble onto his crotch, but Dieter moved it to safety. He pulled a letter from his case and flourished it like a magician waving a scarf performing a trick, handing it to me as if I was a small child he was trying to entice.

I picked up the letter and started to read: "Dear Mr. Kraus. Further to our telephone conversation, my client, Mr. Richard Burton, agrees to take part in your movie *Vergeltung* for the sum of fifty thousand U.S. dollars." It was signed Maurice Klotzky, attorney at law, Geneva, Switzerland.

I held onto the letter, saying, "Richard Burton for fifty thousand dollars! Wow!" Seeing the name Richard Burton—the actor that I most admired—was like telling me that God was going to star in the movie.

I handed the letter back and Dieter returned it to his case. My feelings changed toward him, but I still had questions. "He gets at least seven hundred and fifty thousand dollars a picture, if not a million by now," I said. "Fifty thousand wouldn't even pay his bar bill."

"That is exactly why he will accept it," Dieter said. "Richard Burton is a dead horse in the Hollywood derby. A drunken dead horse. Nobody will hire him because of his drinking."

"Then why should we?"

"His lawyer says he is finishing at a health clinic. This means he is drying out. If we move quickly, we can make the film when he's on the way up again and by the time we're in release, he will be as big as he used to be. Assuming he stays sober—and we will make sure he does."

"I see." I was still cautious. "And you're going to direct?"

"Of course."

"With all due respect, Doctor Kraus—"

"—Dieter—"

"—his career's already in the toilet. Do you honestly think he's going to let a first-time director pull the flush?"

"Everybody has to start somewhere. Why should it not be at the top?"

His arrogance—he sped past self-confidence when he snapped his fingers at the waiter—was astonishing. I had to admire it. "Your plan sounds great," I said. "You almost convinced me. But in a few weeks I am going to be a father for the first time. I simply cannot afford to work on spec. The diapers alone will put me in the poorhouse."

"The moment I have money, I will pay you. I promise."

"The baby won't wait."

"Am I not speaking to Yoram Ben-Ami?"

"What are you saying?"

"The same Yoram Ben-Ami who fooled Otto Preminger into hiring him by saying that all the People of Israel loved him for making the film *Exodus*?"

"Where did you hear that?" I asked, surprised.

"Word gets around. Your reputation precedes you. You had great nerve then. What do you call it? Hootspa?"

I corrected him. "*Chutzpah.*"

"Do you have enough chutzpah left to help me with another film?"

He had me. I didn't want to say yes, but there was something about this kraut's manner that made me think he might actually pull it off, and if he did, then perhaps I might have a chance as well. "I will consult with my wife," I said.

Just then the waiter presented the tab and set the tray down before Dieter. Dieter was unfazed. "Why don't you get this one, Yoram."

I laughed. "Now which one of us has the 'hootspa'?"

"If we are to be partners—"

Neither of us moved. Then Dieter took out his wallet and placed a ten shekel note on the tray. "All right, this time I get the check. I will charge it to the film."

"We don't have a film," I reminded him.

He slapped his billfold closed and pocketed it. I swear it sounded like he was clicking his heels together. "We will!"

* * *

Ani, my beautiful wife, was less than thrilled when I reported my meeting with Dieter Kraus: "Are we going to have this baby on spec, too?" We were standing in the washing machine section of an appliance store on Tel Aviv's Dizengoff Street. I wanted to buy her the best machine to handle the expected diapers, but the best costs money we didn't have.

"Can't your agent get you a real job?" she said.

"Ani, really," I said softly so the salesman couldn't hear. "I don't have better offers," I said. "I don't have any offers, period."

"I have an idea," she said. "Maybe we can buy a washer-dryer on spec."

This is why I love her. She went back to looking at the washers, lifting the lids one by one and avoiding my eyes. I swear I saw her tell one of the washers, "I married a dreamer! He wants to work for free."

Playing along, I lifted up the lid of the washer next to hers and told it, "Tell her we still have enough to live on. Tell her she'll see. I'll come out of this an international producer."

"More pie in the sky," she said to her washer.

I turned so my head was next to hers and added, "This pie has Richard Burton in it."

The salesman saw us with our heads in the same washer. "You picked out the best one," his spiel started. "What month are you in?"

"Eight months," Ani said, touching her stomach. Her smile made me forget our disagreement.

"This can easily handle a week's load of cloth diapers," the salesman continued, nodding toward Ani's belly. "And it draws no more electricity than a television set."

"We don't have a television set, either," Ani said more to me than to the salesman.

"In that case, he said, "after we look at the washer-dryers I'll be happy to show you some television sets."

"How much is this unit?" I asked.

The salesman brightened. "It's affordable. And if it isn't, we can always work out a payment plan."

"That's already too much," Ani said. "Do you have anything second-hand?"

"Come back in a year," the salesman said, his smile dissolving. "By then it will be second-hand." He walked away.

"This is my big chance, Anushka." When I wanted to reach her, I would speak to her as though she was still a little girl named Anushka. "It's our big chance. No more small-time Israeli pictures. No more local TV shows. No more strapping scenery on the top of our car or bringing our furniture to the set. This is the big-time."

Ani shifted her weight from one foot to the other. "Who's this Dieter Kraus?"

"He's a dermatologist but he's also produced documentaries. Now he wants to direct theatrical features. I think he comes from money.

He dresses like it. No frayed cuffs. I just need this chance, Ani, this one chance. *We* need it." I patted her tummy. "The *baby* needs it."

"I don't like you working for free and neither does the baby. When would you start?"

"I think I already have," I shrugged.

* * *

Two days later we started spending Dieter's seed money by renting a room in Jerusalem's prestigious King David Hotel to use as an office. It's a trick I learned from Otto Preminger. If people think you're rich, they will give you money. A truck arrived at the hotel with filing cabinets, chairs, desks, and other office equipment and we were furnished.

I was labeling folders when Dieter burst into the office holding a Telex. (Before e-mail and faxes, offices communicated internationally by a kind of typewriter called telex.) He was all smiles.

"He wants to come!"

"Who wants to come?"

"Richard Burton. Look. He says he wants to come and get a feeling for the locations and speak to us about the script."

"Why?" I asked. "We don't need him until we start shooting, and we can't start shooting until we have the money."

"Don't you understand?" Dieter said, pacing excitedly like a puppy about to be walked. "Richard Burton in Switzerland gets us nothing. Richard Burton in Israel gives us legitimacy. We bring him here, we make nice, we keep him away from the booze, we have him take pictures with the politicians, and that gets us in the newspapers. Perhaps we can get him to agree to shoot a five-minute promo reel on these locations that we can show to investors and distributors to prove he's not drunk. We tell the press and everybody wins."

"Good," I said. "We have a saying in our family: 'if you dress for the job, you will get the job.'"

"And we have a saying in Germany," Dieter said. "*Wenn du mitt den Adlern ficken willst, musst du wissen, vie man fleight.*" He read my blank stare correctly. "In other words, if you want to fuck with the eagles, you'd better know how to fly."

* * *

My first task making the Burton visit happen was getting an official invitation from the government of Israel. To do this, I called on Nathan Goldstein of the Israeli Film Center. I knew him from my previous productions, but this was a big moment for me. He was the public face of Israel's film community, always showing up in handshake photos with foreign stars and international filmmakers. His office was a library of guide books, tourist brochures, catalogues, and scrapbooks of past productions shot in Israel. Oddly enough, above his desk, rather than a collage of stills or even a map of the country, he had hung a color photograph of the Dead Sea.

A beaming Goldstein and his secretary listened to my request. "The whole film?" he said, impressed.

"Six to eight weeks," I assured him. "Every foot of film will be shot right here in Israel."

"This is good for the economy and jobs for our crews," he said, motioning for his secretary to start pulling forms for me to fill out. "Looks like you're really moving up in the industry, Yoram."

"Before I go, I'm going to need a couple of things from you in this office," I said.

"Anything. Permits? Work papers? Visas?"

"First things first," I said. "I need an official invitation from the State of Israel. We're going to bring our star here for location scouting and advance publicity and I want to make as big a deal out of him as possible. He's a huge star."

"Of course," Goldstein nodded. "Who is it?"

"He's one of the greatest actors in the world."

"Who? Who is it?"

"Every woman on earth knows who he is." I teased.

"You've got me hooked," Goldstein said, excitedly. "Who is he?"

I stiffened my spine and said, proudly, "Richard Burton!"

Goldstein hit his forehead with the palm of his hand. "*Oy vey!*"

"*Oy vey* what?" I asked, suddenly concerned.

"*Oy vey* Richard Burton!"

"What do you mean? What's he done?"

"Never mind what he's done. The answer is no."

I was both confused and surprised. "Is he officially banned? Is it because he's played Nazis? I promise you, he was only acting."

"No, not that at all," Goldstein said.

I was getting worried, "You're not going to try to keep him out of the country, are you?"

"No, let him come, have him do whatever he needs to do. But he can't be an official guest of the State of Israel."

"Why not?"

"Just believe me. No."

I wouldn't let this go. I had to know. "I can't believe you're turning down one of the biggest stars in the world."

"I'm not," Goldstein said. "I'm turning down one of the biggest *shikkers*—drunks—in the world. He's a pain in the *tuches*."

"He's huge!"

"A *huge* pain in the *tuches*, then. He used to be a star, now he's a drunk. It's no secret. If I send an official invitation to Richard Burton they'll say I was drunk too. I'll get fired."

I was beside myself. Bureaucrats! I looked quickly around the office. I had to make a point about how stupid this was. My eyes fell on the picture of the Dead Sea over Goldstein's desk. I pushed my way behind the desk and ripped the frame off the wall.

"*This* is what this office is here for?" I held the frame in front of Goldstein's face. He tried to brush it away but I moved it back. "*This* is what you show off to visitors who come here to make movies? The Dead Sea?"

"What about it?" he said, squirming away. I could see his secretary reach for the telephone.

"The Dead Sea?" I drove it home. "You should have a picture of you hugging Richard Burton. Even drunk, he looks better than the Dead Sea!"

I'd made my point. I tossed the framed picture aside and walked out of the office.

"You want him here so bad," Goldstein called after me, "bring him here on your own. In a bottle."

I slammed the office door as I left. Through it, I could hear Goldstein tell his secretary, "This guy's *meshugeneh*!" Maybe I was. But even a meshugeneh can still have ideas.

I walked out of the building into the main street and crossed to the King David which is across from the Israeli Film Office. The meeting with Goldstein left a big hole in our plans, something I'd have to work around. I like overcoming obstacles. Each of them is a personal test. I started to feel like I always feel when I am pushed to the wall. Whenever that happens, I come alive like a boxer who is being hammered by his opponent. Being pushed to the wall makes me fight back and get creative, not defeated. By the time I entered the King David Hotel lobby I already had my trick ready. I smiled at its potential and made a beeline for the concierge.

"I'd like to send a Telex overseas to Switzerland," I said. The concierge took up his paper and pencil.

Dictating, I said, "'To Mr. Richard Burton, care of Maurice Klotzky, Attorney-at-Law, Geneva, Switzerland. We are happy to invite you to be our guest of honor in Israel. Arrangements will be forthcoming. Thank you very much.' And sign it 'The State of Israel.'"

The concierge's pencil hand froze on the paper. "*The State of Israel?*" he said with a full display of doubt on his face.

"Maybe you're right," I backtracked. "Better sign it "The State of Israel and its film industry."

"Excuse me, sir, but I can't send that. Are you saying that you're the State of Israel?"

"Aren't we all?" I smiled and walked toward the elevators.

"And your room, Mr. Israel?" he called after me.

"Bill it to room 252."

3

IN THE UPSTAIRS LIBRARY of Richard Burton's home in Celigny, Switzerland he sat in his favorite chair reading a book while Taylor reclined on a chaise lounge slugging her way through *Vergeltung*. At first she just shook her head in amazement. Then she gave an occasional sigh. Finally she resorted to tongue-clicking, after which Burton could no longer ignore her.

"What on earth is that sound you're making?" he asked.

"This script," she said. "I keep waiting for it to get better."

"You're an optimist," Burton offered dryly. "At first I thought it was the translation, then I realized it was always that way. Still, I've done worse."

"I guess you'll just have to hold your nose and think of the tabloids."

"Please, Elizabeth," Burton said, finishing his third soda water in an hour, "I'm already shaky enough."

"Sometimes you just have to bite the bullet," she said. "When I was a little girl at Metro, Mr. Mayer would tell me, 'Elizabeth, I need you to do me a favor and be in this picture.' And of course I'd do it because I loved Mr. Mayer and I knew he always looked after my best interests." She could see Burton's mind wandering and reached over to touch his hand. "I always knew you looked after my best interests, too."

"We don't need the money," he said in his rumbling voice. "Maybe I should bow out."

Now she was in her element. When Elizabeth Taylor set her mind to do something, it got done. "This isn't about money, darling, it's about us. We're the Lunts of Hollywood. America doesn't have royalty, they have movie stars. We're Hollywood's royalty."

Burton made no response. He continued to brood. Taylor perked up. "Hey, have you read the part of Katrina in this script? What do you think I could do with it? What do you think these people would do if I wanted to play her?"

"The word *plotz* comes to mind," Burton said, giving a distinguished twist to the Yiddish expression for "collapse." "They would absolutely, totally, and completely *plotz*."

She crossed from the chaise lounge to sit at his feet. He always liked it when she did that. "If I did, I could be with you, we could be with each other, and together we could keep the supermarket checkout lines stocked for a year. What do you say?"

Burton laughed heartily. "I'm ashamed I didn't think of it first."

* * *

When I returned to our small production office in the hotel I didn't want to bother Dieter with Goldstein's stonewalling or the Telex I sent to Klotzky. As a matter of fact, Dieter was on the phone to Geneva with Klotzky and was apprehensive that his star had changed his mind. Actors are mercurial, after all, and who knew if sobriety had made Richard Burton reconsider.

"Is everything all right with your client?" Dieter asked the attorney.

"Yes, he's fine, he's in perfect health and more dedicated than ever," Klotzky assured him. "But there's another matter I'd like to discuss with you."

Oh God, thought Dieter, here it comes. Perks. They want to stay in a private home or have their own chef or who knows what? "What can I do for you?" he asked hesitantly.

"I was wondering if the role of Katrina has been cast yet," Klotzky said.

This did not surprise Dieter. He was smart enough to predict what would come next—and it did. "No, it hasn't been," he said.

"In that case, I was wondering whether you might consider Miss Taylor to play her?"

Dieter checked his hearing. "Would you mind repeating that, please?"

"Certainly," the lawyer said. "Would you consider Elizabeth Taylor to co-star as Katrina opposite Richard Burton in *Vergeltung*."

Klotzky didn't even have to finish his sentence before Dieter said, "Yes!"

"Fine. Would you make arrangements for her to accompany him to Israel?" Dieter managed to stammer another "Yes" before hanging up amid profuse thanks. He signaled me to sit down, then gestured for me to stand up. He was smiling ear-to-ear and had stars in his blue eyes.

"It looks as though we are going to have to spend a little more of my seed money, Yoram," he said, trying to keep his news from bursting out of his chest. I thought about keeping quiet to see what would happen, but by this time I, too, was curious.

"Why?"

"You'll never believe it."

"Try me."

He practically did a ballet around the room as he repeated the news. "Can you believe I am going to direct Richard Burton and Elizabeth Taylor in my film?"

"*Our* film," I corrected, and noted, with no small amount of disbelief in my voice, "and do you really mean that the two biggest stars in the world are coming to help us publicize a movie they think is already financed?"

Dieter's smile did not fade. "I did not tell the lawyer that."

"When were you planning on telling them that we're going to use them to raise the money and that you are going to be the director?"

"Let's get them here first. Meanwhile, how's our money holding out?"

"*Your* money," I corrected playfully. "Remember that we have to spend money to make money."

"The eagles are flying, all right," he said.

I started calculating in my head. "This changes everything. Forget the Film Office. I'll call Mayor Kollek directly. He loves to be on the front page with celebrities visiting Jerusalem. He'll place the whole city at our feet."

Dieter's smile suddenly fell off. "How much more will this cost us with limousines, guards, flowers, more hotel rooms—?"

"I'll find out," I said, heading for the door. "I have to reserve more rooms here. I'd better do it in person."

As I left, Dieter called after me, "Make them separate rooms. Burton and Taylor are not married any more, you know. The last thing we want is a scandal instead of publicity. We are not making *Cleopatra*." Then he called out, "And get a discount."

Few people who stayed at the King David ever thought of asking for a discount. It was like buying a Rolls-Royce; if you had to ask how much it costs, you can't afford it. Guests were above such crass inquiries, and the breadth and stature of those guests were part of its majesty. A five-star-hotel built out of pink marble in 1931, it stands fortress-like over Jerusalem. Sternly overlooking the Old City and Mount Zion, it has hosted royalty, diplomats, tourists, and journalists (on expense accounts, to be sure). It was also the site of a bombing in 1946 and, in 1959, one of many locations used by Otto Preminger for the filming of *Exodus*, to note two extremes in its history.

Its elegant design incorporates traditional Eastern-style arches, domes, and colored stones. The public areas feature religious symbols and inscriptions, and the guest rooms, designed by Swiss architect G. G. Hufschmid, evoke a variety of cultures including Assyrian and Phoenician, while incorporating modern conveniences. In addition to conference rooms of varying capacities, it boasts four dining areas ranging from simple poolside snacks to the elegance of the La Regence main dining room.

Its vast lobby looks like the set from a Cecil B. DeMille biblical film. High ceilings, lush draperies, a polished marble floor, framed paintings, and geometric archways painted with old world symbols make it look like a royal palace. As I walked across its expanse on the way to make the additional room reservations, I encountered the hotel's resident manager, Ilan Fink. He was pacing and seemed to have the weight of the world on his shoulders. The moment he saw me he rushed over to offload some of it onto mine.

"I don't have good news for you, Yoram," he began, "but you and Mr. Kraus are going to have to leave the hotel."

This caught me by complete surprise. "Why? What have we done?" I asked defensively.

"It has nothing to do with you. In fact, I have to cancel your reservation for Richard Burton as well."

"You're not making sense," I said, trying to salvage our project. "Tell me what's happened."

"It's out of my hands," Fink said.

"What's out of your hands?" Now I was getting angry. "Start at the beginning."

"It isn't just you, Yoram. It's everybody. We have to clear the entire hotel for Henry Kissinger's visits."

"But you're the manager. How many rooms does Kissinger need?"

Fink sighed at having to repeat the explanation he must have given a dozen times already that day. "You don't understand, Yoram. American

Secretary of State Henry Kissinger is coming here in August for peace talks. When Kissinger stays here, the Americans take the whole hotel. The King David becomes a security zone. The place is occupied by the Diplomatic Security Force, the CIA, his staff, his press, TV crews. They all have advance security clearance. All of that is what it takes to try and make peace between the Arabs and Israel, to make diplomacy work. We're relocating everybody. I'll try to find you rooms at some other hotel. I'm sorry."

I searched for some kind of counter-argument. The King David wasn't just any hotel; it was a seal of approval. I decided to become dramatic. "Do you realize what this means?" I said, putting my hand to my forehead. "My people can't stay just anywhere. They always stay here when they visit Jerusalem, even if they've never been here before."

"What are you talking about?" he said. I had managed to confuse him.

"There's no other hotel in Jerusalem that even comes close to this. It isn't just the prestige, it's your very operation. You're the only hotel that knows how to be a true international hotel."

"Tell you what," the manager said, trying to pull away. "If we ever do a TV commercial, you can write and direct it. And maybe act in it. Meanwhile, I'll make it up to you. I'll even comp you for your office—which you have to get out of by ten o'clock tomorrow morning, by the way."

At that moment something I have since called Yoram's Luck clicked in. The chime on the lobby elevator rang and three men walked out: a neatly dressed older gentleman and two stocky, younger men. I recognized the older man as Joseph Sisco, Undersecretary of State to Henry Kissinger.

I immediately left Fink behind and ran across the lobby to Sisco. I shouted, "Mr. Sisco! Mr. Sisco!" as I hurried toward him. Both of the younger men stepped in front to block my way; they turned out to be his bodyguards. "Mr. Sisco," I said, "I am an Israeli film producer and I am making a movie with Elizabeth Taylor and Richard Burton. Do you think that Mr. Kissinger would mind they stayed in the hotel with him?"

"Not at all, not at all," Sisco said, and kept moving.

By this time, Fink had closed the gap and was standing next to us. I turned to him triumphantly. "Did you hear? Did you hear?" I said. "We're gong to stay in the hotel." Sisco smiled and left with his bodyguards. Just to seal the deal, I said after him, "By the way, Mr. Sisco, you look better in person than on TV." He made no response.

Fink and I stood alone in the empty lobby. I was all smiles but Fink was angry. "Yoram, I really don't like what you just did to me. This is really chutzpah."

"No," I responded. "Chutzpah is that I am going to ask you a favor: to give me two extra rooms for Elizabeth Taylor. And do it for a discount."

* * *

For the next hour in our now-re-established production offices, I worked the phones while Dieter watched in amazement. If you have the nerve, you quickly find that desperation and opportunity make a remarkably successful combination. My plan was this: with the Kissinger party arriving from Egypt—surely at Ben-Gurion Airport just outside of Tel Aviv—I had to arrange the Taylor-Burton flight from Switzerland to land in Israel as close to the Kissinger arrival time as possible. In that way, the press that would normally be on hand to cover the Kissingers would also be there to cover Burton and Taylor. It was complicated by the fact that Kissinger would be arriving on a United States plane that would have run of the air space and airport for security reasons. But that didn't mean that it would be unscheduled. It was a small task to call Ben-Gurion Airport and learn when the runways and air space would be locked down for a "charter" on the 27th.

Built as an airstrip in 1936 by the British and transferred to the newly formed State of Israel in 1948, its name was changed from Lydda to Lud and, by the 1960s, had grown to welcome over a dozen international air carriers. Its name was formally changed to Ben-Gurion Airport in 1973 to honor our first Prime Minster, David Ben-Gurion.

Unlike what it has become, the airport in those days was a simple, accessible compound where passengers and their loved ones could walk onto the tarmac to board and deplane. Despite the unusual security concerns of the Middle East, it was nothing like what it has unfortunately become in modern times. That's why it was so easy to learn the arrival schedule of the Kissinger flight by simply asking. A call to Swissair reserved first-class seats for Taylor and Burton on a flight which, by our luck, was due to land at about the same time. We were also informed that Taylor would be bringing, at her expense both for travel and to stay at the hotel, a bodyguard and a woman who did her makeup for public appearances.

The rest—limousines, advisements for coverage, extra security, etc.—was up to Dieter and me, although we worked with the Bureau of Diplomatic Security that protects the Secretary of State and other diplomats while abroad. Thanks to Sisco's consent, they were agreeable.

4

IN THE MIDDLE OF ALL this, Ani gave birth to our son, Dory, at Hakira Hospital in Tel Aviv. Forget Liz and Dick; Ani and Dory were the only stars in my universe as I sat beside them in the hospital bed. I could do nothing but stare into his beautiful face. He was gorgeous and dark like his mother with captivating eyes and a personality that was already bursting out of his baby blanket. Of course, I might have been a bit biased.

"Blessed are You, Lord our God, King of the universe, who is good and bestows good," I said, repeating the traditional *HaTov VeHameitiv*.

"Look at him," Ani said softly. "Does he look like us or not?"

By then I had already made the requisite inventory. "He's all there," I reported, "ten fingers, ten toes, and a bulbul. I guess I'd better set up the bris."

There was a knock on the hospital door and, to my surprise, Dieter entered. This was a surprise, but a welcome one that showed his concern.

"I have come to offer my blessings," he said. "How do you say in your language? *Mazel Tiv?*"

"*Mazel Tov*," I offered, "and thank you."

"Is it a boy or girl?" he asked.

"A boy," Ani said.

"And of course you'll be coming to the *brit milah*," I said.

"What is a *brit milah*?" Dieter asked.

"I don't know what it would be called in your language, but in English it's called circumcision." He had the expected reaction. Most non-Jewish men, when they hear the word *circumcision* and realize what it is, cross their legs whether they're sitting or standing. Dieter was too German to be obvious about it, which I appreciated, but inside I knew he was reacting protectively.

"*Wunderbar!*" he managed. "What are you naming him?"

Said Ani proudly, "We're going to call him Dory."

"Dory?" Dieter looked puzzled. "That's the name of a kind of fish." I looked it up later. He meant John Dory, also called a Blue Tang. (How would he know that twenty-eight years later "Dory" would become a Disney character—something our son has had to deal with ever since *Finding Nemo* came out in 2003.)

"What would you propose to call him?" Ani cautiously asked.

"I'd give him a normal name," Dieter said, "like my son."

"What is your son's name," Ani asked.

"Fritz. It's simple."

"Fritz is a normal name?"

"It is for me. Who do you know named Dory?"

Ani didn't give an inch. "Our son."

Dieter handed me a check. "What's this?" I asked. "It can't be salary."

"Unfortunately, no," Dieter said. "It's for the baby. For his college account."

I looked more closely at the name on the check. "Who's Fritz Ben-Ami."

"Just think about it," Dieter said. I handed the check to Ani.

"Thank you," she said genuinely. "Yoram says you're a doctor."

"A dermatologist."

"But you make films?"

Dieter softened. "I wanted to please my parents. I went to medical school, graduated, and faced the prospect of setting up a practice where all day long I would squeeze people's pimples. I couldn't face a life of that, so I decided to become a filmmaker. Do you think I'm crazy?"

Ani considered this for a moment before answering, "Yes." Dieter looked shocked. Then she added, "But anybody is crazy who wants to give up a stable profession to live the life you want to live."

"I told you she was a special woman," I said to Dieter.

"In that case, maybe we're all crazy," he said.

I looked at Ani and Dory and said, "Let's hope it runs in the family."

* * *

A few days later, Burton and Taylor were scheduled to arrive. Dieter and I were at Ben-Gurion two hours ahead of time in case the plane landed early. I dug my two-year-old wedding suit out of my closet and dressed up to meet the flight. This was an exciting moment for me; I was going to meet two big international stars. Dieter and I discussed ways of delaying our guests' deplaning until the Kissinger flight also arrived. We set up at the terminal well in advance of any reporters. I brought a bouquet of mixed flowers to hand Miss Taylor. Dieter had prepared presskits about *Vergeltung* to distribute to reporters. A public relations mainstay, these presskits contained a plot synopsis of the script (ending just before its pulse-pounding climax), biographies of Burton, Taylor, and Dieter (I didn't want mine included, arguing that nobody knows me), a general press release about the importance of having these two stars appear in the film, and a piece praising Israel as the perfect location to shoot the picture. Dieter must have included his name and the title of the film half a dozen times on each page. I was going to say something to him about this, but I figured that it was his film, he was raising the money, he wanted to direct, and I was just a hired hand. That feeling was to change over the next few days as events spun in a different direction, but let me tell the story the way it unfolded.

First the plane arrived carrying Secretary of State Henry Kissinger, his wife Nancy, and their press and State Department entourage. It was a sleek Boeing C-137 Strat-o-Liner modified and operated by the U.S. Air Force. It had "United States of America" emblazoned across its side and landed heavily on the tarmac, slowly rolling to a stop in a sequestered area as if to let anticipation build. It stopped a fair distance away and was met by limousines and members of the American Embassy in Israel, but its doors remained closed. One surmised that Dr. Kissinger was holding court inside to the press corps that traveled with him.

1975 was the thick of Kissinger's celebrated Mideast diplomatic talks designed to bring peace between the rival factions, one of which was Israel, and the others which seemed intent on pushing us into the sea. Everyone called it "the peace process" but what it really meant was that Kissinger, representing the Ford Administration, kept shuttling from one hot spot to another in an attempt to quell differences—as if the actual players were incapable of doing so on their own. The charming and shrewd Kissinger, one of the world's most controversial figures, was known to seduce the press with his intellect, which he was no doubt doing on the plane while the ground-based reporters waited with growing impatience for the door to open.

Meanwhile, Burton and Taylor's flight landed from Zurich and taxied to its own spot on the tarmac a short distance from the terminal. The ground crew met it with a stairway that they rolled into place. Watching both planes on the field and glancing at the journalists chomping to be let loose on them, Dieter turned to me and said, "The reporters are going to have to make some hard choices whom to cover."

I held open the airport door for Dieter, who was clutching his presskits, and walked to greet the Burton/Taylor plane. We had leaked strategic information to the Israeli media and they had leaked it to the public so that, as we looked back at the terminal, we could see hundreds of people holding huge banners stretched across its windows reading "Shalom, Liz" and "Welcome Liz." The fans lined up politely inside the terminal waiting to catch sight of her. No guards or barriers were there to stop them, only their respect for her.

We, of course, were more eager to see Burton than Taylor. Dieter, in particular, burned to get him aside in private and glean his input into the script. Disgraced and unemployable as he might be, he was still Richard Burton, the acclaimed English actor, the longest running Hamlet in Broadway history, the wit, the man in whose mind were held the greatest passages of Shakespeare, Milton, Keats, Coleridge, Joyce, Thomas, and who knows how many other great writers?

But it was Taylor whom the public yearned to see, particularly in Israel. Born in England in 1932 but achieving fame in America, she notably converted to Judaism in March of 1959. There were reports that she converted so she could marry her fourth husband, singer Eddie Fisher, a Jew, in May of that year. But she had not converted in 1957 when she married her third husband, the successful Jewish showman Mike Todd. She converted, she said, because of her regard for the Jewish people. This was the first time she had visited Israel, but it was still an emotional homecoming on many levels for many people.

The reporters were caught in the middle. Torn between the importance of the Kissinger story and the glamor of Taylor and Burton, the press made the most prudent, proper, and professional choice.

They headed for Liz and Dick.

In the meantime, Dieter and I had clamored up the airline stairs and into the first class section of the Swissair jet. As we had arranged when we booked them, Burton and Taylor sat in the first seats in the first-class cabin. A young man, Jason, their bodyguard, sat behind them, along with a woman who was lifting a makeup case from underneath the back of Taylor's seat. Other passengers disembarked, passing the famous couple and pretending not to notice them. Burton and Taylor, practiced in such drills, were neither rude nor aloof, but prevented any embarrassing moments by carefully avoiding eye contact with anyone but Dieter and me.

"On behalf of all the people of Israel, welcome to our country," I started, and handed the flowers to Miss Taylor.

"Indeed," she said sweetly, then glanced out the window. "All of the people of Israel seem to be outside waiting for us."

"It's an honor meeting you," I said, and introduced myself. "I'm the producer, Yoram Ben-Ami. I'll be in charge of your schedule while you're here."

Dieter stepped forward, juggling the presskits while trying to shake hands. "And I am Dieter Kraus. I appreciate your coming and I look forward to discussing with you—"

I interrupted Dieter before he got the chance to say he wanted to direct. "I am also a great fan of your films." I confess that I couldn't help myself. Actors are one thing but stars are another. They truly are different.

The makeup lady began primping Taylor's hair and touching up her face. While she did, Taylor asked Burton, "How do I look?" He nodded in approval. Then she turned to me. "How do I look?"

I heard myself say, "More beautiful than Cleopatra." It must have landed well because neither she nor Burton reacted negatively or, for that matter, at all.

I did notice that Burton's face was moist, something I first attributed to the warm, enveloping August evening that was blowing in from the open door. But he was also tightly gripping Taylor's hand on the arm of the airplane seat.

On board the Kissinger plane, Undersecretary Joseph Sisco finished his briefing to the Secretary and Nancy Kissinger as they gathered themselves and prepared to deplane.

"Have you finished with the onboard reporters, Henry?" Sisco asked the Secretary.

"I have. What's the status of the foreign press?" Kissinger queried.

"We have your microphone set up and waiting for you."

"Very good, Joe," he said in his German-accented English. "How many are there?"

"Well, Henry, there's a small problem there."

"What's that?"

"There's plenty of press but they'll all covering Elizabeth Taylor and Richard Burton."

Nothing throws Henry Kissinger. "I expected as much when you told me they'd be staying at the hotel," he said glumly.

"Do you want me to ask them to relocate?" Sisco said.

"Certainly not," Kissinger responded. "I can turn this to advantage."

"What shall we tell the press traveling with us?" Sisco asked.

Without having to think about it, Kissinger said, "Tell them that we are pleased to share the limelight with Miss Taylor and Mr. Burton, and that their presence here is symbolic of the optimism that we all have for the successful outcome of the peace talks."

While I remained with our stars, Dieter walked carefully down the stairs and into a waiting gaggle of reporters, all of whom were looking past him for some sign of the famous pair.

"Here is the full press material," poor Dieter said, trying to quiet the reporters with little success. "You know that Mr. Burton has arrived in Israel to see the locations for *Vergeltung* in which he agreed, to my great delight, to play the lead. I can also announce that Miss Elizabeth Taylor will star opposite him. Again, the picture is called *Vergeltung* and I am honored to say that I shall be directing it—"

Dieter held out the presskits for the reporters to take but not one of them was interested. He tried again. "We have full information in the press material if you would take it and look at it please. This is an important moment for all of us. I do hope we will have a press conference at the King David Hotel once Mr. Burton and Miss Taylor have settled in."

It was no use. Rather than hear Dieter's spiel the reporters regrouped around the stairs to watch for Taylor and Burton.

Inside the plane my concerns were confirmed when Taylor lifted Burton's hand from her arm and said to him, softly but reassuringly, "We can do this." The makeup lady stowed her wares, and Jason stood up to clear the way.

We stepped into the Israeli evening lit by the floodlights of a dozen cameras and the flashes of a score of others. Taylor grasped the flowers; Burton held onto her and the railing. I stood behind them, and beside me was Jason carrying an attaché case. I offered to take it for him but the moment he saw my hand reach for it he yanked it away, said "I'm good" firmly, and then added "thanks" with a tight smile. What on earth could be in it?

As we descended the stairs, the cameras started rolling. Taylor, carrying my flowers, wore a blue and white pantsuit, head scarf, and dangling earrings. Burton descended beside her wearing a khaki safari suit and red trousers. I nearly stumbled on the stairs, blinded by the lights. Taylor was used to it. She waved to the crowds. They shouted "Shalom! Shalom!" back at her with increasing fervor. Others shouted "Elisheba," her biblical name when she converted to Judaism.

Across the tarmac Henry and Nancy Kissinger and their party stood forlornly and practically alone at the open door of their limousine. They looked at the brouhaha surrounding Taylor and Burton. Nancy looked at her husband as if to say, "What's the matter Henry?" although she already knew the answer.

"They prefer Liz and Dick to me. Do you know how this makes me feel?"

The only appropriate answer—but it was not in Kissinger's lexicon—would have been "humble."

Sisco intervened. "The press is ready for you, Mr. Secretary." The Undersecretary led Kissinger to his microphone where a handful of reporters stood ready to hear him. There was also a small podium on which the moderately diminutive (five-foot-nine) master diplomat stood. As he spoke, most of his audience was distracted by the cheers welcoming Taylor. When they thought the Secretary wouldn't notice, some even turned their heads to catch a glimpse.

"Could we have a few words about how the talks are going, Dr. Kissinger?" one of them asked.

"The gap has narrowed," Kissinger said. "It will continue to narrow."

"Do you think you will finish soon?" asked another. All softball questions.

"I do not like to negotiate on the basis of a deadline. I have said I am hopeful and I shall continue to be hopeful."

The next question was more pointed. "Mr. Secretary, Israeli Foreign Minister Yigal Allon has been quite specific about details of the Sinai accord you're here to work on. Specifically, he spoke of the deployment of Egyptian troops—"

Kissinger interrupted. "I don't think I can share his views now. We shall have an opportunity to discuss the problem in detail at a later stage."

"Would you advise Mr. Allon to stay silent?"

"I would not like to prevent others from speaking on every conceivable subject before the night is over," the diplomat said, and the tarmac exchange was over.

By now even Kissinger realized that Taylor and Burton were the show, not him. He and his party piled solemnly into their limousines.

Likewise, Taylor, Burton, Dieter, Jason, the makeup lady, and I got into one of the limos we had rented for the term. The second limousine carried their luggage. There were eight pieces: one each for Jason and the makeup lady, four for Taylor, and two for Burton. Why two people would need six suitcases and trunks for a four-day visit escaped me. Then again, I am used to living out of a shopping bag if I have to. Laden with luggage, the second limo followed ours to the hotel.

"Thank you so much for coming," Dieter repeated once we were on our way to Jerusalem.

I intervened, cautiously. "Let's get you settled at the King David. After that we have arranged a short press conference."

Silence struck the car. Burton took a look at Taylor, and then, his voice a bassy rumble that left no doubt that he meant it, said, "I don't do press conferences!"

You could cut the tension with a knife. I felt I had to say something to break the silence. "Whatever you want, Mr. Burton. I'll make the announcement." Then, in case he might respond to guilt, I offered, "I'm afraid the people of Israel will be disappointed."

Taylor seemed to take this as a cue and took Burton's hand. "Oh, come on, Richard. You can pretend to be charming for a few minutes, can't you? After all, that's what we're here for."

Burton sighed in surrender and gave her a slight nod of the head. She interpreted it for us: "We'd love to."

5

ILAN FINK ASSIGNED OUR PARTY the Presidential Suite. Frankly, I would have preferred that Burton and Taylor get the Royal Suite because I considered them royalty.

The Presidential Suite was beyond impressive. It was bright, enormous, and overlooked the Old City and the Tower of David. It had two large bedrooms connecting through a spacious living room that was so well appointed with a desk, chairs, and a convertible sofa bed that I immediately claimed it as my office. Naturally Burton would have one bedroom and Taylor the other; the propriety of doing otherwise wasn't even a discussion. However many husbands Taylor had had or would have, the fact is—and her friends attested to it—she was a one-man woman and her ardor was, with the sole apparent exception of her *Cleopatra* romance with Burton, confined to the marriage bed.

Every amenity had been imagined and put in place by the hotel staff. There was a room fridge stocked with only soda, orange juice, and water as I had instructed; no alcohol. There were trays of candies, nuts, and small cakes. The moment Fink opened the suite door we were overwhelmed by the fragrance of flowers. It was so strong that it crossed the line into odor. "Good Lord," Burton said when it hit him, "it smells like Kew Gardens in summer." Taylor accepted it as her due, although she did look at a few of the cards on the flower sprays and cast them casually aside.

"I thought everybody planted trees in Israel," Burton said offhandedly, "not flowers."

"I think they're lovely," Taylor pronounced.

The luggage had already been brought up and Taylor's makeup woman, who apparently also functioned as an assistant, began unpacking them. No sooner had we shut the door to the suite than the telephone rang. Asserting my control, I answered it, "Vergeltung productions." It was *The New York Times* calling from New York asking for an interview. I knew he wasn't interested in speaking with me.

I pressed the receiver against my chest. "It's *The New York Times*," I told Burton. Before I could say anything else, he waved them off and stage-whispered back at me, "Why do you think we're doing a bloody press conference?" I then had the pleasure of telling the *Times*, "I'm sorry, but Miss Taylor and Mr. Burton will be holding a press conference shortly and it will be their only statements during their trip." Burton nodded in approval. Then I added, "But of course you're free to send a photographer for their public appearances." This earned a conspiratorial smile from Burton.

I hung up the phone but, no sooner had the handle hit the cradle then it rang again. I told *Newsweek* the same thing: "Sorry, no interviews." Within the next five minutes I said repeated it (with increasing pleasure, feeling my importance) to *Time*, *The Guardian*, and the Australian *Daily Telegraph*. Burton eyed me with what I hoped was approval. Taylor stood at the window peering out at the city.

"If *News of the World* or the *National Enquirer* should call," Burton said, "let me know."

"You mean you actually *want* to talk to them?" I asked, incredulous.

"Lord no," Burton laughed, "but I think it would be fun if you held the phone up while Elizabeth and I blew them a razzberry."

"Be careful, Richard," Taylor said, turning around. The backlight from the afternoon sun created a halo around her head that made her look beatific. "Or they'll print that Liz and Dick have flatulence."

"As you see," Fink interrupted clumsily, trying to get on with his managerial duties, "we have separate rooms for each of you. Miss Taylor is over here in this suite and Mr. Burton is over here in this one. Mr. Ben-Ami will set up an office in the living room between you."

"Which of you is Mr. Ben-Ami? Burton asked.

"I am," I said. "Yoram Ben-Ami."

"What may I call you?"

"Yoram, if you want. Or Benny if you don't want to remember Ben-Ami." I waited for Burton to say "Call me Richard" but no such permission was forthcoming. Miss Taylor, of course, would remain "Miss Taylor."

Dieter offered, "And you may call me Dieter. I wonder if we might discuss the project while you are getting settled." Taylor brushed him aside politely but effectively. "I'm terribly tired from the flight. Perhaps we could go over everything tomorrow."

"As you wish," Dieter agreed reluctantly. He turned to Burton, who didn't give him a chance to ask the same question as he picked up his own suitcases and went off into his bedroom to change. I motioned to Dieter to hold off.

Burton was changed in a matter of minutes in preparation for the press conference but Taylor, ever the star, took her time. I called the hotel switchboard and instructed them to put all calls through to me, and then only those that sounded official, diverting the others to messages. As we approached an hour's wait for Taylor, an increasingly impatient Dieter drew me aside.

"He is just standing around," Dieter said of Burton. "Why can't I talk to him now about the movie?"

"He's nervous about the press conference," I tried explaining. "It's like a stage performance. You're a director; don't you know how actors get?"

"How long do you think she'll take? The reporters won't wait forever."

I had to shake my head and grin. "Of course they will."

An hour and fifteen minutes later we took the elevator to the press conference. Taylor looked dazzling. When she entered the room you could feel the power of her stardom push everybody a foot back. Not physically, but emotionally.

The main ballroom of the King David was bursting with reporters beyond its seating capacity when our group arrived; I am sure that fully half of the press should have been covering Henry Kissinger. It was raucous with tension as well as excitement. The excitement came from the presence of two great stars. The tension hovered because everyone knew that Burton hated talking to the press and, even when he did, he never spoke about himself. A trail of misquotes, presumptions, and insults from the Fourth Estate had sealed his mouth. Often explaining that he could stand negative comments hurled at him but not those that were aimed at Taylor, he bridled, in particular, at pronouncements that he might have been a truly great stage actor "if only he hadn't been seduced by Hollywood." For this reason he asked us to announce to the assemblage ahead of time that personal questions were off limits (not that any reporter worth his ink would have obeyed such a command). Dieter was thrilled, however, because it meant—he hoped—that the entirety of the confab would be about *Vergeltung*.

"Look at all this publicity!" he said as we saw the crowd. "It's got to be worth millions of dollars!"

Taylor and Burton stood clear of the lectern to allow the photographers to take their flash pictures. Burton was by now wearing a black shirt and black jacket, and Taylor was dazzling in a green and white caftan, pendant necklace, and her hair covered slightly by a scarf. By now the photographers were popping flash photos; the barrage was painful and dizzying. How could they stand it? Dieter ate it up, no doubt imagining himself at the film's world premiere. The pair stoically ignored disrespectful shouts from the paparazzi of "Over here, Liz!" and "This way, Dick!" until Taylor gestured for silence.

"First," she began, "I'd like to thank the government of Israel for inviting us." The room went wild with applause while Dieter and I tried to keep from blushing at my lie inviting them on behalf of the government of Israel. "Next," she continued, "as a Jew, I have waited fifteen years to visit this country. If I had known you'd be throwing us this kind of welcome, I wouldn't have waited so long."

That did it; any heart that she didn't melt with those words had to be made of stone. It remained for Burton to put a pall over it by saying, with his sheer authority, "Thank you all for being here, but let me advise you that we shall not answer any questions of a personal nature."

Taylor immediately tried to change the subject by saying, "We're looking forward to seeing the holy sites."

The next question was to be expected: "How has all the press coverage you received affected your professional and personal lives?"

"Oh really now," Burton said, making any response impossible.

Taylor added, "Bravo! Sneaky."

Not to be topped, Burton said, "You write the questions and I'll write the answers and you can read them when I'm dead."

Taylor took charge and recognized another reporter. His question: "How long will you be here?"

"Just a few days. It seemed natural to come here. He was coming on business, so we combined business and pleasure."

"What holy site are you most interested in?" the same reporter followed up.

"Oh, the Western Wall, of course," Taylor said, respectfully referring to it by its formal name rather than the "Wailing Wall." "Of course, I just want to breathe the air and feel the sun." She then called on another reporter.

"Did you bring the diamond?"

Only then did I notice Jason, standing behind Taylor, stiffen. "Yes we did," she said, indicating Jason, "and I also brought along a very large and well-trained guard." The room laughed at her response and she recognized a man sitting near the rear of the hall.

"Miss Taylor," he began, "what is the significance of your coming here with Mr. Burton. After all, the two of you divorced a year ago."

"Another sneaky one!" she shot back, then apparently thought better and added, "We were both invited and thought that—"

Burton interrupted her. He threw her a momentary glance, and then said, "As a matter of fact, there is significance. It is the one personal question I shall answer." The room buzzed in anticipation. "I have proposed marriage to Elizabeth and she has accepted. It is our intention to have our wedding here in the Holy Land."

The room exploded with more flash pictures and more shouted questions. This scoop caught Dieter and me unprepared. I saw his face flush. In a matter of seconds, Burton had wiped any possible interest in *Vergeltung* from the press conference agenda.

"You mean *re*-married," a reporter corrected, standing in the center of the room.

Said Taylor in her most charming manner, "I tried very hard to be divorced but it doesn't work for me. I like to be married."

"To the right man," Burton chimed in.

"And this is why we'll do it again," Taylor finished.

The reporter remained standing. "It's good publicity for you, is it not?"

"We don't care about the publicity," Taylor offered with straight face. Portions of the room murmured in disbelief.

"You *are* Jewish, of course," the reporter continued, getting at something.

"Yes," Taylor said, her smile becoming forced. "As everyone in this country seems to know, I converted in 1959."

"Why did you convert?"

She tossed her head back—her raven-black hair was contained by her scarf—and said, "When I learned of the Holocaust I was appalled at the suffering of the Jews, and I was overjoyed at the birth of the State of Israel. I was drawn to their heritage—your heritage, really—the more I studied. I had instruction for nine months under Rabbi Max Nussbaum at Temple Israel in Hollywood."

"Is that an Orthodox Temple?"

"No, it's Reformed," she said.

The reporter wouldn't let go. "So it wasn't because of your marriages to Mike Todd, whose real name was Avrom Goldbogen, or Eddie Fisher, whose real name was Edwin John Tisch."

"No," Taylor said coldly.

"Nor changing your own name to Elisheba Rachel?" he said, pronouncing Rachel as "RAY-chul."

"Elisheba Rachel," Taylor countered, pronouncing it in the Hebrew "rah-HCHEL."

Burton stood in anger. "I *resent* the inference in your question, sir," he began, using his Shakespearean voice to nail the man where he stood. "Elizabeth is *not* an opportunist. It might interest you to know that, at the same time she converted, she purchased *one hundred thousand dollars* in Israel Bonds—"

"I didn't mean to—" the reporter attempted to apologize, but Burton was on a tear.

"—for which she and her films were *boycotted* by several Arab countries. She has faced discrimination in buying a home, and she is marked because she is sympathetic to Israel. If *that* doesn't make her a Jew, then I misunderstand the evil of anti-Semitism!"

The room fell silent. Taylor used the moment. "I never really feel like a Jew until somebody attacks me for being one." She then nodded to me, rose from her seat, and told the room, "thank you all for coming."

Jason went ahead to secure an elevator that was being held for us by the Diplomatic Security force and we rode back to the Presidential Suite. Dieter and I were the last to enter, and he turned to me, still armed with his presskits, and said, hurt, "They didn't mention my movie." He left.

* * *

Burton entered the suite grumbling, "You wanted a bloody press conference and you got a bloody press conference."

"I wanted a press conference, not an excommunication," she said. "That was quite a performance you gave down there."

"Perhaps now you know why I avoid such opportunities."

"But sometimes they can be useful," she said and winked. (I should have known there was a message hidden in that wink.)

"Excuse me," I said, using the momentary silence between phone calls to point to the flower arrangements that were still arriving. "Who's sending all these? I think I'll have them put in the hall." I signaled a bellman to move everything out.

The telephone rang again and I screened the call. "How do you feel about *People*?" I said.

"It depends on the individual," Taylor said playfully.

"I mean *People* magazine."

"Do we get the cover?"

"Do they get the cover?" I asked the caller. He said "no promises" and I repeated it for Taylor. She gave it a thumbs-down.

Burton started looking through the telephone messages that had been left on the table. "Look, my love, the Kissingers have invited us for a late dinner. But if you're tired I'll send regrets."

"Nonsense," she said, perking up. "I'm not tired."

To Burton, I said, "Tomorrow Teddy Kollek, the mayor of Jerusalem, has offered to take us around to see the sights. We can talk about the project then. How does that sound?"

"Splendid," he said, and headed off to his room without so much as glancing at Taylor or saying goodbye to me. Miffed but covering, she turned to her bodyguard, Jason.

"Jason, open the case. I'd like to wear 'it' to dinner." The young man rolled the combination lock on the attaché case and flipped up the top. Inside, cushioned in foam and covered with plastic, was the Cartier Diamond. I couldn't take my eyes off it. Not only could it have financed our movie, it could have lifted the fortunes of three or four Third World nations.

Discovered in a South African diamond mine in 1966, cut into a pear-shaped gem weighing 69.42 carats, it was purchased at auction by Burton as a gift for Taylor in 1969 for $1,050,000. Taylor had it mounted as a pendant on a diamond necklace and wore it only on special occasions because of insurance concerns. Seeing it in person after hearing about it was mesmerizing. Then, as casually as one would lift a pecan off a nut tray, Taylor scooped it up in her hand and took it with her into her rooms.

The phone rang again. This was no longer amusing. I answered it sharply, "This is Yoram Ben-Ami. What do you want?"

"Yoram, take it easy," the caller said. It was Ani. "When are you coming home?"

"How did you know where to find me?" I asked.

"Are you kidding?" She said. "I called the hotel and they put me right through. It isn't like there are that many famous people staying there. Will you be home tonight?"

"I'm not sure," I said. "I don't think so." As we spoke, I sifted through the message slips that Burton had been reading. All except the one from the Kissingers were from fans who wanted to pay their respects or shady operators who wanted to sell them something or crazy people outside who think they looked like them. "I have a lot of detail work to handle."

"How can I reach you?"

"Call me by name at this extension. I'm going to have the switchboard block all incoming calls except yours and a few others. Otherwise we'll never get anything done."

"What room are you in?"

I couldn't avoid the truth. "I'm staying in Burton and Taylor's suite, the Presidential."

Ani laughed as only she could do. "You're bunking with Liz and Dick?"

"They don't like to be called that."

"Oh excuse me. When they come over for tea I'll be careful."

"No," I insisted, "I really am staying in their suite. But don't worry, we all have separate bathrooms and I have my own bed."

"Yoram?" she said.

"Yes?"

"I miss you. I want you here."

After Ani and I hung up, I made up the rollaway bed in the center connecting room. I searched the closets in the suite for bed linens, spare pillows, and other accoutrements. The suite was beyond description for a kid who grew up in a kibbutz with sand roads and a socialist ethic. I wondered what the poor people were doing tonight. Then I realized that I was one of those poor people who also happened to be staying in the Presidential Suite of the King David Hotel in Jerusalem two floors away from Henry Kissinger and twenty feet away from Elizabeth Taylor and Richard Burton.

6

THE ROYAL SUITE AT THE King David overlooked the Old City and the lighted glory of the Tower of David. Burton and Taylor were seated at an intimate dinner table on the patio with Dr. and Mrs. Kissinger. It was high enough above the ground that the bugs didn't venture up to bother them. Taylor wore the Cartier diamond around her neck so, naturally, the conversation centered on it.

"It only adds to your beauty," Kissinger said, his German accent unaccountably making him sound gentle.

"Thank you," she said, "but I can only wear it thirty times a year or the insurance company has a fit. The rest of the time my bodyguard sleeps with it."

"Yes, one learns to ignore bodyguards," the Secretary said. Then he asked Taylor, "What's it like being the most famous couple in the world?"

Burton took the question. "I was about to ask the two of you the same thing."

Kissinger grinned. "Nancy says that I'm the famous one and she's only along for the ride."

"That would be my answer, too," Burton said, looking at Taylor.

The waiter arrived with the wine. Kissinger approved it, and then the waiter poured for his guests. When the waiter got to Burton's glass, Taylor covered it with her hand.

"Richard is being a good boy these days," she told the Kissingers proudly.

"Although I'm still a bit shaky," he said.

"He needs to get back to making films."

"I've often wondered," Burton said, changing the subject, "how do you deal with a head of state who regards diplomacy as weakness? When does statesmanship venture into brinksmanship?"

Kissinger considered for a moment and then said, "Let me avoid answering by quoting you a line from one of your films, the one in which you played the Archbishop of Canterbury."

"That would be *Becket*," Burton said proudly.

"King Louis of France has a line that I have never forgotten, and it applies here. Speaking of his testy relationship with King Henry of England, Louis says, 'Crowned heads can play the little game of courtesy but nations owe one another none.' In diplomacy one sometimes needs to get past the Man to see the Mankind."

"Is there anything you don't know something about, Dr. Kissinger?" Taylor asked with all her charm.

Kissinger smiled with all of his. "I don't know." Everyone laughed. Taylor raised her wine glass, took a sip, and then glanced at Burton who was playing with the stem of his empty glass.

"Let me tell you something about Man and Mankind," Burton said, looking at his glass rather than into anyone's eyes. "Perhaps I shouldn't say this at all, but about a year ago I ventured as close as I'd ever come to the edge. For a moment or two I thought about leaping off."

"You mean taking your own life?" Kissinger said.

"Well, you see, I saw how splendid life was and how undeserving I was of it."

"Richard was consuming two bottles of hard liquor a day," Taylor confided.

Burton went on, "I started to drink because I was ashamed of being an actor." He gave a tight smile, still not looking up. "The critics sometimes agreed."

"Yeah, critics, what do the critics know?" Taylor said dismissively.

"Strangely enough," Burton continued, "I get equally angry whether I am praised for my work or damned."

"What galls me is when the idiot critics write how great an actor he *could* have been if he hadn't gone to Hollywood," Taylor griped.

"Is there a better reason to drink than Hollywood?" Burton said, pulling the mood out of the abyss. "I'll tell you a secret. All actors are insecure and stars are worse. We are—" he searched for a word that would be accurate without sounding egocentric, "*—different.*"

"I'll drink to that," said Taylor, raising her wine glass.

"I won't," Burton countered, upending his empty glass so the opening was on the tablecloth.

Taylor became serious. "Dr. Kissinger, why do you think that you can make peace between Israel and Egypt when no one else has been able to do it?"

Kissinger was unequivocal. "Because I believe in it."

Burton leaned toward the Secretary. "We both practice brinksmanship, Dr. Kissinger, just different kinds. Godspeed to us both, eh? *Prost!*"

"Cheers," said Kissinger.

* * *

The first thing Jason did when Taylor handed him back the diamond after the Kissinger dinner was proceed to the hotel safe and see that it was locked securely inside. Not that he expected anyone to steal it; the King David was literally brimming with armed diplomatic security people. But as a foreign, non-governmental visitor, he was not permitted to carry a firearm into the country, and he had to assure the insurance company that it was being protected. Jason was good at his job. Young, fit, and uncannily observant, other Hollywood celebrities considered it a coup that Taylor was able to engage his services, which included advising others on protection. I would come to admire this man even though he made it a point to stay aloof from everything except his job.

* * *

The next day we met Teddy Kollek, the mayor of Jerusalem. Kollek, then 64, smiled and held out his arms as he welcomed the Burton-Taylor party. He had arranged a tour shuttle to take them through Jerusalem. A separate press pool shuttle would follow, its seating having been decided by lottery.

Called "The Mayor of all Mayors" by New York Mayor Ed Koch, the highly popular Kollek was a pioneer in the statehood struggle for Israel. Before that, during World War II, he used his wiles and his Viennese passport to save the lives of hundreds of Jews threatened by the Third Reich. David Ben-Gurion pushed him to run for mayor of Jerusalem in 1965 (he would serve until 1993) and, once elected, he worked to improve and unify the city, making it a home for Muslims and Christians as well as Jews.

The tour of Jerusalem that Kollek was about to give us would be his second of the day. His first was performed alone. He was celebrated for driving around the city every morning at dawn looking for potholes, burned out traffic lights, and a myriad other details to fix to make his city grow and shine.

I had the honor of presenting Burton and Taylor to Mayor Kollek. "Finally," Taylor said, taking his hand with both of hers and sealing her acceptance forever, "I've heard so much about you."

"And I have certainly heard about you!" Kollek winked.

"Then I look forward to showing you the truth," Taylor joked as we got into the van.

"Let me show you my beautiful, historic city," Kollek said, and proceeded to do just that. The tour was an unforgettable experience. Naturally I had seen Jerusalem countless times before but, like New Yorkers who can live in their city all their lives and never visit the Statue of Liberty, I was stunned with how much of the Holy City I had missed growing up.

To the east of Jerusalem, along a high ridge, lies the Mount of Olives. Rich with history, it was once covered with olive trees. King David escaped over the Mount of Olives when his son, Absalom, rebelled in *2 Samuel 15:30*. This is also where wise King Solomon built a pagan shrine for his foreign wives (*1 Kings 11:7-8*), and where Ezekiel saw the Lord ascending from the city and stopping there (*Ezekiel 11:23*). It is also where Jesus foretold the Second Coming in the New Testament. Teddy Kollek was conversant with all such history as our tour went to this popular location.

Next we drove to the Jaffa Gate, one of seven entrances to the Old City of Jerusalem. Built in a shape to confound attackers, it leads to the Christian, Muslim, and Armenian Quarters. It is also the access to the Temple Mount.

Easily the most coveted and controversial site to Jews, Muslims, and Christians, the Temple Mount is where the First Temple stood until it was destroyed by the Babylonians in 586 B.C. Occupation of the site has shifted among the leading sects for centuries and it is fastidiously guarded and revered.

If you can imagine making small talk with big stars, that's what we tried to do as we drove around the city. Correction: Dieter and I tried to make small talk. The only one who did it successfully was Mayor Kollek. A lovable man, he was always at ease with people of accomplishment because he had so many accomplishments of his own. He could also be a movie fan. When he asked Taylor about making *Cleopatra*, she diplomatically deflected it by saying, "I really don't remember much about making *Cleopatra*. There were a lot of other things going on," (such as her romance with Burton and her near-fatal case of pneumonia). She did tell him something I thought was most revealing, however, and it's a lesson I have tried to practice the rest of my life. As is well known, Taylor and Burton's romance during the shooting not only created rifts in both their marriages, it lit a fire that helped sell the film. The personal fallout, however, was profound. As Taylor put it, "You find out who your real friends are when you're involved in a scandal."

During the entire Kollek-Taylor exchange I kept my eye on both Burton and Dieter. Burton ignored Dieter, preferring to gaze away from him out the window. Dieter, seeing him doing that, looked as though he wanted to get his attention to discuss the script. I didn't have any trouble realizing that the reason Burton kept looking out the window was so he wouldn't have to engage Dieter.

Finally, Taylor said, "Some of my best leading men have been dogs and horses." At this, Burton turned toward her with mock irritation.

"Where does that leave me?"

This earned him a kiss. "In a class by yourself."

I watched Kollek's reaction. He kept a politician's straight face even though he was watching a kiss between an unmarried man and woman, something unacceptable in Orthodox Judaism.

Our tour turned down David Marcus Street. Before us loomed a sandstone colored building that was a mixture of biblical classicism and modern. It was the Jerusalem Theatre, a four-stage structure dedicated to the performing arts. "It's our newest theatre," Kollek said. "I had the honor of opening it in 1971. It seats just under a thousand in one auditorium and decreasing amounts in the other three. It was funded almost entirely by Miles Sherover and was designed by Michael Nadler. It has already emerged as a showplace for all sorts of productions."

"The building looks beautiful," Burton agreed.

"By the way," Kollek said, "I understand that you're considering giving a performance for us there."

"Really?" Burton said. "Where did you hear that?"

"I read it in the paper," Kollek reported. "Surely someone told them."

"That sounds like my lawyer jumping the gun," Burton said. "I'm afraid that cannot happen. He's been trying to get me back on the stage. It's a bit premature for that, I think."

Kollek wasn't giving up. "Perhaps you'll reconsider once you get more of a feel for the city and its people. You've seen the reception everybody is giving you. A performance would be wonderful. Even better: a *benefit* performance. Word would spread like wildfire and I bet we'd sell out in an hour."

"I'm not really prepared," Burton hemmed. He didn't sound like he was being modest or that he wanted to be talked into it. It sounded like a clear but polite "no."

"Oh, I bet you have a repertoire of classics stored in that marvelous mind of yours," Kollek flattered him. "I bet you could go on as Hamlet at a moment's notice."

Then the truth came out. "Perhaps, but, you see, I haven't been on the stage in years. It's a very different thing, appearing in films. No one outside of the crew sees your failures. A live audience is a living, breathing, unforgiving animal."

Kollek shook his head, but he hadn't given up completely. "A pity. In one night you could help us raise enough funds to finance an entire season of plays so every child in Jerusalem, Arab and Jew, could see one. How old were you when you saw your first play? Shouldn't you want to inspire some other young Richard Burtons?"

Burton avoided further comment and went back to staring out the window. "It is a lovely building," he said flatly as we left it in the distance.

We drove another twenty minutes along the circuitous Hebron Road until we approached Ma'ale HaShalom Street. This was the closest we could drive to what was the purpose, at least for Taylor, of the day's excursion. Her eyes grew moist with the meaning of where we all were. Kollek noticed and spoke in a soft voice.

"We are now approaching one of the holiest places in all of Judaism. This is the Western Wall of the Old Temple. It was destroyed by the Romans in 70 A.D. People also call it the Wailing Wall or the Kotel. When we step out of the van to go there we will have to separate. Men and women cannot mix here. And please cover your heads in respect for Hashem." He handed each of the men yarmulkes from a bag in the van and we emerged into the bright sunlight.

No sooner had our eyes adjusted than who accosted us but Nathan Goldstein, the overly cautious bureaucrat I had tangled with at the Israeli Film Office. He had a photographer in tow and proceeded to make an instant pest of himself. Obviously he couldn't ignore what he had seen across all the media from the moment the famous couple arrived in Israel.

"Mr. Burton," Kollek said, "this is Nathan Goldstein who runs the Israeli Film Office." Burton shook his hand blandly and looked at me for instructions. I shrugged.

"I'm so pleased to meet you," Goldstein enthused. "I'm glad you could come." While his photographer snapped away, Goldstein kept positioning himself next to Burton and Taylor to the exclusion of Kollek. Kollek, no fool, knew that Goldstein was trying to increase his own prominence and countered him at every move. It was a comic ballet. Finally Goldstein said something that nearly made me laugh in his face: "I'd like you to know that the State of Israel welcomes you and wants to do everything to support your movie." I could see in Goldstein's eyes the goal of getting embraced by Burton so he could replace the picture of the Dead Sea behind his desk. When he tried to grab Burton, however, Burton backed off as though he had been attacked. Goldstein, thus rebuked, then regrouped and said, "If it's okay, I would love you and Miss Taylor to fly with me over Israel in a private plane and avoid these crazy crowds. Perhaps tomorrow?"

"Thank you," Burton responded, "but I need to check with Miss Taylor—and, of course, with the man who's in charge of our schedule. You know Yoram Ben-Ami, don't you?"

Goldstein's jaw hit the ground when Burton deferred to me. I was happy enough that Burton remembered my name, but it felt even better to be able to give the unctuous Goldstein a dig.

"We've met," I said flatly. Goldstein was bested, and backed off.

We made quite the tourist group. Kollek, Burton, Dieter, Goldstein and his photographer moved toward the men's section while Taylor and Nancy walked toward the women's section. Jason the bodyguard and I accompanied the women, God forgive us, for safety.

Much to our dismay, the press, largely male, followed Taylor and Nancy to the women's side of the wall. Jewish law is strict about mixing men and women at worship. It must not be done lest the presence of women distract the men from their sacred obligations. This prohibition was trampled by the journalists who dogged Taylor and Nancy as they attempted to pray, show their respect, and leave messages.

One of the customs of visitors to the Western Wall is to leave prayers written on small slips of paper inserted into cracks in the wall. Whether this invokes divine presence or defiles this most holy of sites has long been debated. What people don't fully realize when they leave these intensely personal messages in the wall is that each evening they are pulled out of the cracks and tossed, unread, into trash bags by the rabbi in charge, and disposed.

Kollek, Burton, Dieter, and Goldstein encountered minimal press interest as they walked respectfully to the men's side. I must admit that Burton and, especially, Dieter looked odd in their yarmulkes, or skullcap.

On our side, however, there was mounting chaos. While hundreds of women worshippers surrounded them and called out "Elisheba! Elisheba!" the press—particularly those with cameras—kept saying, "Over here, over here." Taylor was used to ignoring the press but it threw Mrs. Kissinger. Jason and I tried flanking aside the onrushers but we found ourselves being driven against the two women we were trying to protect. At the same time, the other women at the wall were screaming, "Only women here! Only women! Men out! The men have to get out!" Their words fell on deaf ears, or rather, ears that couldn't hear for all the hubbub.

"What's happening here, oh my God" I heard Taylor say. Remarked Nancy, "This is awful. Just awful!"

Hearing them was the red alert. I shouted across them at Jason, "Call security. It's time to get out of here. We'll be killed." He was already on the walkie-talkie contacting the Diplomatic Security force that had been guarding the men.

"We have to evacuate now," he said. "Reassemble at the van. Repeat, evacuate now."

"Everybody back to the van," I echoed.

"No," Taylor said. "I have to make it to the Wall. That's why I came here. Please, let me pray." Beside her, Nancy Kissinger was swept along in the crowd which was both surging forward and pulling our group to one side. Taylor put her head down and forced her way through, being fiercely jostled every step of the way. She was determined to leave her slip of paper. We tried to protect them both. It was August, it was hot, it was humid, and the level of excitement was as suffocating as the weather. Finally, inching forward, the women managed to touch their foreheads to the Wall and put their rolled-up prayers into its tiny crevices.

"Let's get out of here," Nancy said, and we hurriedly withdrew. The shoving on the way out was as upsetting as it had been on the way in.

On the men's side, Burton managed to reach the wall, press his forehead against it, and back away without incident. Dieter respectfully approached the Wall and offered a prayer, then waited. At that point, their bodyguard heard our distress messages and urged the party to leave.

"We need to get out of here and join the others. Come on."

Once clear of the plaza, Taylor and Mrs. Kissinger, their clothing ruffled, dove into the waiting van and the rest of us followed. The driver closed and locked the door and took off, trying not to hit the photographers and onlookers who surrounded us, jockeying to peer inside.

Burton held a sobbing Taylor in his arms. "All this chaos," he said softly to her. Then he turned to Dieter and me and barked, "This better well help your film!" He embraced Taylor and tried to soothe her. Soon her anger overcame her fear. "Did you see them?" she said with disgust. "Oh, it was horrible. All I wanted to do was pray."

"Such a shame," said Nancy Kissinger.

Kollek was stunned and apologetic. "I've never seen anything like this," he said. "I'm sorry."

"The men following us into the women's side!" Taylor said. "I've never seen such disrespect, not for me but for the other women who were there."

"You're with me now, dear heart," Burton said, holding her tighter.

"I just wanted to pray like any other Jew."

Burton looked at her tenderly. "But you're not any other Jew."

7

WHEN WE RETURNED TO THE hotel there was already a BBC radio report on the room music system. The announcer was saying, "Liz and Dick's visit to the Western Wall was the scene of a near riot this afternoon. Seeking to gain attention for their flagging careers, the world famous movie stars visited the holy site and drew major crowds. Almost immediately, the crowds started to riot as—"

"Turn that thing off!" Taylor commanded. "Jesus Christ, turn it off."

I killed the radio and Burton walked Taylor into her bedroom. "Shh, shh, it's off. Now get some rest."

"I've never in my life been so afraid," she sobbed. "I don't want to go anywhere ever again."

"You need a good night's sleep," he said. He helped her to her room, opened the door, and stood there while she walked slowly inside. He did not follow her in. Instead, he closed it and turned to Dieter. "Would you leave us alone?"

Dieter reluctantly left the suite.

"Do you want me to leave too?" I asked. Burton shook his head "no" and kept silent until Dieter had gone a few paces down the hall. "You can stay."

Burton ran his fingers through his hair and looked out over the Old City. It was dusk and the lights were just coming on. "I suppose it's nice to be popular in the holy land," he said dryly, "I just wish we weren't this popular." He turned to me. "Are you staying here again in this little room tonight?"

"Yes," I said. "I live in Tel Aviv but it's too far to go and get back in the morning."

"Are you married?"

"Yes," I said, "and my wife just had our first child."

"You should be with her," Burton counseled.

"My wife says the same thing."

"What do you want to do?" he asked. It took me a long moment to decide.

"I think it's better if I stay here."

"Very good," Burton said. "Now let me give you some advice." He went to the largest and most beautiful of the many floral displays in the room, removed the to/from card, and reached into the desk for a piece of note paper.

"Tell your wife that Elizabeth and I are demanding your presence here and that, rather than disappoint us, you're staying on a roll-away in the living room." As I wrote, he picked up the room phone. "This is Mr. Burton in the Presidential suite. Would you be so kind as to send a bellman to pick up flowers for personal delivery to Tel-Aviv. I'll have the address for him when he gets here." Then he turned to me. "Write your address on the back." I did. Burton took the note and address, clipped it to the flowers, and turned it over to the bellman when he came and handed him a bill drawn from his pocket without looking at it. "I believe the expression is 'Say it with flowers,'" he joked. "Even with somebody else's flowers, the words are still yours." With that he went into his own room and closed the door.

I made up the sofa. As I was settling in, Burton's bedroom door opened and he exited in pajamas and carrying a toothbrush. "Good night," he said, as he passed without looking at me, and headed straight into Taylor's bedroom, locking the door.

"I was wondering if you were going to show up," Taylor teased Burton.

You may ask how I knew what was going on in their bedroom. At first I tried to be discrete and cover my ears, first with my hands, then with a pillow. That lasted about ten seconds before I told myself, "Don't be an idiot. This isn't your mother and father fighting in the next room, it's Elizabeth Taylor and Richard Burton! Some day you may be able to tell about it. Open your ears and listen!" So I flung aside the pillow and enjoyed the show.

"I wasn't sure you wanted me to come in after what happened today," Burton said. "Of course, if you're too addled, I'll leave."

"Nonsense," she said dismissively.

"No, I mean it," he persisted. "After all, if getting slightly jostled while trying to pray makes you want to cancel all public appearances while we're here, we might as well go back to Switzerland."

"*Slightly jostled*?" she said. "I was practically knocked down at the Western Wall while you were hanging around with the guys pretending to be religious."

"Pretending?" he said, raising his voice. "I have that within which passeth show."

"Oh don't quote *Hamlet* at me," Taylor said sharply. "I'm the one who's Jewish. You're only Welsh."

I recognized the line from *Hamlet*, too. Their voices carried from the bedroom to the living room. Hearing two articulate people argue is always fascinating, like a traffic accident where you see it coming but don't want to look away. If the combatants are both actors who know how to make dramatic points, the excitement is beyond description.

"The Welsh are almost Jewish," he said. "We've had our share of persecution. And don't change the subject. You and I are here to be seen, and you want to hide."

Shifting position on the sofa bed, I missed a few words, but it wasn't hard to hear Taylor shout, "Famously frail? What's that supposed to mean?"

"It means, dear heart, that you're in hospital more than you're in front of the cameras."

"How dare you make any comment at all about my health? I've seen more death's doors than you've seen bottoms of liquor bottles."

"Yes, dear heart, but I don't call the press every time I celebrate."

"Celebrate what, and don't you dare call me 'dear heart.'"

"Celebrate liberation from you. In case you wonder why we got divorced it was because we couldn't stand each other."

"And now you want to get re-married because why?" she hissed. "Because no other woman will have you except me?"

Burton exploded. "Is this a sympathy marriage? Is that what you're trying to say? I don't need your bloody sympathy."

"No, you can get sympathy from any woman you charm into your bed. And the way you've been performing lately, you'll need charm."

"That's a desperately sick lie," he said.

"Now you're quoting *Who's Afraid of Virginia Woolf?*" Taylor said. "Very good, Richard. You've shown your range from Shakespeare to Albee. Isn't there any Burton left?"

I didn't recognize the quote until she mentioned it. This was getting good.

"There's plenty of Burton left," he seethed. "He's looking for the remnants of the monument to self-absorption otherwise known as Elizabeth Taylor."

"If I'm concerned about myself," Taylor said defensively, "it's only because I've learned that I have to look after myself."

"Here it comes again," Burton mocked, talking to her as though she was a child. "Whatzamatter, itty-bo, did big bad Hollywood steal your soul? Or did they buy it with a long-term contract, pampering, and stardom?"

"Just because I made it in Hollywood and you didn't—"

"Don't you dare," Burton warned. "If you so much, as put a toe into the fetid waters of the 'he could have been a great actor if he hadn't made movies' swamp I swear I'll take your Oscar for *Butterfield 8* and—"

"You know I made that trash to get out of my MGM contract. The Oscar was for my other work."

"The Oscar was because you survived your tracheotomy during *Cleopatra*, dear heart, and let's not kid ourselves."

"Now who's telling desperately sick lies? You're just jealous because you never got one, and now you never will. Or do you think you can pull it off with this piece of crap you've dragged me here to promote? What the fuck is *Vergeltung* in English? And who the fuck is this German director who's never made a movie in his life?"

"It was you who insisted on coming with me to Israel," Burton corrected, "and if you're going to spend all your time sequestered in this hotel, even that will never happen."

She grew silent, then said, "At least apologize for 'famously frail.'"

Now he grew silent. "All right, I apologize for 'famously frail.'"

Neither of them made another sound. I don't know for sure what they did next, although my imagination has its suspicions, but no performance of any kind could possibly have surpassed the one they gave as the overture. Hearing nothing else, I went to sleep.

* * *

Television reports of our Western Wall disaster were just making the late-night news both in Israel and throughout Europe. It took the stations that long to process the newsfilm. I didn't see the reports in my improvised bedroom, but it turned out that Dieter was watching them in his and he was not happy.

"Where is *Vergeltung*?" he shouted at the television set. "What do you think this is all about?"

"Wherever Liz and Dick go, the crowds are sure to follow," the announcer said. "First a busy press conference on their arrival where Burton announced their re-engagement to marry, then it's off to visit the sights of Jerusalem on a personal tour with Mayor Teddy Kollek."

Dieter paced as he waited for his call to go through to Germany, to the offices of Deutsche Cinema Investment Group and its Chairman, Gunter Schmidt. I only learned about this well after the fact, but it's crucial to tell about it here. Schmidt was as irritated at the content of the news coverage as Dieter was.

"The Munich stations are showing the news footage," Schmidt reported. "I see you there in the crowd. It must be exciting."

"We are getting so much coverage," Dieter bragged.

"This is the kind of news we like," said Schmidt. "I cannot tell, is Liz wearing the diamond?"

"To the Western Wall? It would be reckless. Why do you ask?"

"Have her wear it. It would draw more attention. The more attention, the more investors."

"How are the investors coming?" Dieter asked.

"Have her wear it," Schmidt repeated, ignoring Dieter's question.

"It comes with a bodyguard."

"I would like to meet her. Where are you staying?"

"The King David," Dieter said, "but it's on security lockdown because Henry Kissinger is also staying here."

"No problem," Schmidt said optimistically. "Just tell them that I am with you."

"That isn't how it works, Gunter."

"Make it work," Schmidt said. "I'll be there. *Auf wiedersehen*."

"If you come, bring some cash with you. We can use—" but Schmidt had already hung up.

* * *

I swear that I did not eavesdrop on Taylor and Burton's pillow talk but this is the gist of it. As Taylor switched on the light beside the bed, she laughed, and Burton looked at her lovingly.

"I think I've missed your laughter the most," he said. "Depending what causes it."

"Sorry to disappoint you, but I wasn't even thinking of you. I was laughing at the press."

"They amuse you?"

"I bet they'd pay millions to find out what we were doing just now," Taylor chuckled.

"They already do, dear heart. That's what sells papers."

Despite the heat, Taylor huddled under the covers. "They should give us a royalty for every copy they sell. I swear, if I ever need to know anything about my private life, all I have to do is stand in a supermarket checkout line."

"I'm trying to imagine you standing in a supermarket line."

"I'm trying to imagine earning royalties."

"You may have to if this trip doesn't get us onto the covers of at least one tabloid. *The Enquirer*? *The Globe*? *The Sun*?"

"For a man who claims never to read anything they write about us, you certainly know where to look for it."

"It comes under 'Know Thy Enemy,' my love."

"You hate all this, don't you?"

"Yes, but without it we'd be buying those papers instead of selling them."

"You knew the job was dangerous when you took it, Richard. And now you want to get into it all over again?"

"I love the work," he said, kissing her on the shoulder, "but I detest the job."

"What's that supposed to mean?" she said.

"Elizabeth, you are a creature of the crowd. The crowd loves you. I am merely the royal consort."

"Don't kid yourself, Richard. You're part of this."

"A small part."

"Half," she chided. "Don't forget, you're Dick to my Liz."

"A wedding in the holy land," Burton said grandly, sweeping the air with his hand as if describing a banner headline.

"You make it sound Biblical," Taylor said, sinking under the covers.

* * *

I don't know when Burton took his toothbrush and tiptoed past my couch and back into his own room. I also don't know why he had to, except perhaps that they had had separate bedrooms when they were married. Did they care about propriety? I could not understand why any man would leave Elizabeth Taylor in the middle of the night.

That thought was wiped from my head at sunrise when I heard her bedroom door unlock—I was just waking up myself—and then heard her whisper to me. I grabbed the coverlet around my waist, even though I had been sleeping in my clothes, and dragged myself toward her.

The sun was just coming up and so the soft light of dawn lit her face as though by candle. Her negligee hung from her well-known bosom and she stood in the doorway glowing like a movie star. She was only five-foot-two and should have been dwarfed in the unusually tall doorways of the luxury suite, but her presence filled the room like a wide-screen closeup. She didn't even have to say anything in order to captivate me, but she did.

"Yoram? Yoram?"

I rubbed my eyes.

"Would you mind coming into my room for a moment?"

As I entered I told myself that nobody would ever believe me that this was happening.

"I need you to do something for me," she said softly, almost purring.

I looked around the bedroom for Burton. I didn't know that he had already left.

"Don't worry, Richard isn't here. This doesn't concern him anyway."

"Are you all right, Miss Taylor?" I managed.

She walked to the nightstand and turned on the light. All at once she was no longer a creature of the dawn but a victim of a 90-watt white incandescent light. At 43 she was still beautiful, but in the light of the harsh bulb she was, well, Elizabeth Taylor without makeup. . . .

"Yesterday was hell for me, Yoram. Today I don't feel well."

This made my heart skip beats. "Shall I call the hotel doctor?"

"God no," she stopped me. "There would be headlines. My illnesses get more publicity than my films. But you could do something for me."

"Anything." I was putty.

"I can't leave the hotel. I can't go out there again."

"You'll be safe," I said. Boy was I not picking up her hints. "We have all the security in the world."

"You don't understand. You saw what happened at the Western Wall. It will be like that everywhere. I should never have come to Israel."

"Please don't say that," I bit. "The people of Israel love you. The flowers, the banners, the greetings."

"The crowds, the shoving, the disrespect! I'm used to crowds. I'm not used to mobs."

I checked my watch. "There won't be any crowds in the air. At ten o'clock the head of the Israeli Film Office is taking you on a flying tour of Masada in a private plane."

"Masada?" she asked.

"Masada was the last time the Romans attacked the Hebrews in 31 B.C. Rather than submit to slavery, almost a thousand Hebrews committed suicide there."

She recoiled. "That sounds awful!"

"We're pretty strict about false gods and slavery."

"Do I really have to go there?"

"You'll be seeing it from the air," I said. "You won't have any contact with crowds."

"So I really *really* have to?" she pouted.

"I suppose not," I equivocated, "except the Film Office is kind of expecting you."

She took a step closer to me. "Can I trust you?"

"Yes," I gulped.

She suddenly spoke to me in a seductive voice. "I need a big favor from you, Yoram. Can you do that for me? Can you bring me a bottle of vodka? I could really use a bottle of vodka."

"Fine," I said, reaching for the phone. "I'll call room service."

"No!" she shouted. "Let's keep it between us, shall we? You buy it for me. I can't."

"All right," I said, "I'll take care of it."

"Thank you, Yoram. I appreciate it."

I began backing out of her room the way one would exit a meeting with the Queen which, I guess, she kind of was.

"Yoram?" she said as I prepared to leave.

"Yes?"

"A *big* bottle."

Richard Burton (left) playing Winston Churchill (right) in *The Gathering Storm* (British title: *Walk With Destiny*), a 1974 BBC production following Churchill's rise to power at the beginning of World War II. (credit: BBC)

Richard Burton in 1956 at the start of his career when he was predicted to be the next Laurence Olivier—until Hollywood called. (credit: Wiki Commons)

Elizabeth Taylor wears the Cartier Diamond given to her in 1969 by her then-husband Richard Burton who acquired it at auction for $1.05 million. It was thereafter renamed the Taylor-Burton Diamond. Insurance company rules limited the number of times Taylor was allowed to wear it. She wore it in Israel. Her bodyguard kept it in a locked case that he would not let me touch.

Taylor and Burton enter the Jerusalem Theatre for their performance on Saturday, August 30, 1975. I am walking behind them carrying the only bible in the Welsh language in all of Israel for Burton to use in his performance. To Taylor's right are her hairdresser and bodyguard Ziggy Gilboa. Walking in front is Mayor Teddy Kollek. (credit: Zev Radovan)

Secretary of State Henry Kissinger and his wife, Nancy (credit: Wiki Commons)

My Adventure with Elizabeth Taylor and Richard Burton • 73

My wife Ani (right) and me (center) as we were starting our careers in the Israeli film industry. (credit: Yoni S. Hamenahem)

Otto Preminger—sometimes known as "Otto the Terrible"—gave me my first taste of big-time film production when he hired me to be his Israeli production manager on *Rosebud* in 1974. The film didn't do well at the box office but the on-the-job training it gave me proved invaluable. At times I still try to imitate him. (credit: Allan Warren, Wiki Commons)

I'm smiling because I am producing my first American film with director Steve Carver, *Lone Wolf McQuade* (Orion Pictures/MGM, 1983) starring Chuck Norris and David Carradine. The film was number one at the box office and launched my American career. It also led to the highly successful; television series, *Walker Texas Ranger*. (credit: Steve Carver)

The world-class King David Hotel in Jerusalem was where our group stayed even though it was on official lock-down from State Department security because of a "shuttle diplomacy" visit by U.S. Secretary of State Henry Kissinger. Not only the King David but all of Jerusalem opened its doors to Taylor and Burton. (credit: Owen Rozen, Wiki Commons)

My Adventure with Elizabeth Taylor and Richard Burton • 75

Taylor and Burton submit to a press conference at the King David Hotel. It was here that Burton announced that he and Taylor were going to re-marry in the Holy Land. (credit: *Ma'ariv*; courtesy Government Press Office of Israel)

Richard Burton gets testy at the press conference when reporters tried asking him personal questions. "You write the questions and I'll write the answers and you can read them when I'm dead," he said. (credit: *Ma'ariv*; courtesy Government Press Office of Israel)

Elizabeth Taylor and Richard Burton prepare to board the airplane.
(credit: Dutch Photo Service)

Richard Burton and Elizabeth Taylor face each other and the press at the Western Wall. It looks as though all the attention is starting to wear on them; in fact, they crave it. (credit: *Ma'ariv*; courtesy Government Press Office of Israel)

Taylor and Burton on their tour of Jerusalem. (credit: *Ma'ariv*; courtesy Government Press Office of Israel)

The Western Wall, sometimes call the Wailing Wall, the only remaining part of the Old Temple which was destroyed by the Romans in 70 A.D. It is considered one of the holiest sites in all Judaism. (credit: Wiki Commons)

Jerusalem Mayor Teddy Kollek, who held office from 1965 to 1993 and earned the love and respect of millions. New York Mayor Ed Koch called Kollek "the Mayor of all Mayors." (credit: National Photo Collection of Israel; Wiki Commons.)

My Adventure with Elizabeth Taylor and Richard Burton • 79

Elizabeth Taylor and Nancy Kissinger leave the Western Wall after a near-riot caused by crowds and intruding paparazzi. I protected them from the mob with my own body. (credit: *Ma'ariv*: courtesy Government Press Office of Israel)

Elizabeth Taylor and Nancy Kissinger at the Western Wall. Taylor was so upset at being mobbed that she sequestered herself in her hotel room the next day. (credit: *Ma'ariv*: courtesy Government Press Office of Israel)

80 • *Guiding Royalty*

Burton and Taylor have a ceremonial breakfast with Israeli Commerce Minister Haim Bar-Lev. It was meetings like this, rather than discussing our script *Vergeltung*, that tried Dieter Kraus's patience. (credit: *Ma'ariv*; courtesy Government Press Office of Israel)

Taylor and Burton were always being asked for autographs and, in most cases, they graciously obliged. (credit: *Ma'ariv*; courtesy Government Press Office of Israel)

Shimon Peres, who was Defense Minister in 1975 (later Prime Minister and President) invited us all to Sabbath dinner at his penthouse apartment overlooking Tel Aviv. (credit: Elza Fuiza, Wiki Commons).

The Jerusalem Theatre aglow at night in a modern photograph. On August 30, 1975 it was where Richard Burton gave his memorable one-man performance to raise money for youths to see theatre. His special guest star that night was Elizabeth Taylor. (credit: Gilabrand, Wiki Commons)

The historic Tower of David rises above the Old City of Jerusalem. Visiting it was very emotional for Richard Burton, who was a lover of history, in his only visit to Israel. (credit: Wiki Commons)

Elizabeth Taylor (center), Nancy Kissinger (center right) and I (right) during our whirlwind tour of Jerusalem led by Mayor Kollek.

Getting married to writer and script supervisor Ani Nedivi on July 1, 1973 at the Herzliya Film Studios, Israel. (credit: Yoni Hamenachem)

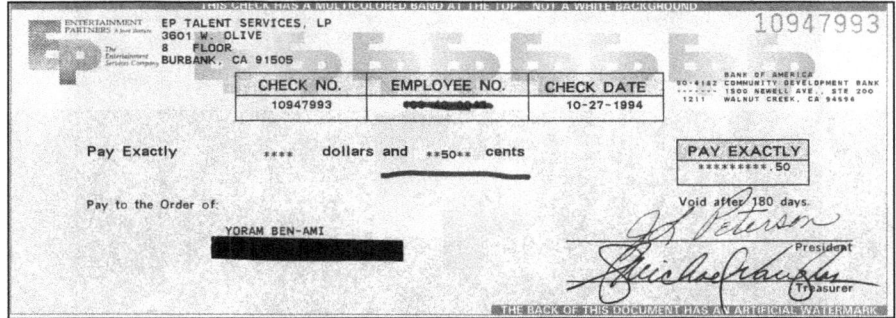

See how it paid to move from Israel to America to become an international producer? Here is a check for fifty cents, my royalties in one of my Hollywood movies. Not to worry; I also had a films that were #1 and #3 at the box office.

Dory Ben-Ami, age four, with his parents Yoram and Ani.

Yoram Ben-Ami

8

THE FRONT OF THE KING David Hotel, even at dawn, was overflowing with people. The Diplomatic Security forces, working closely with Israeli Defense Forces and the Jerusalem police, had set up stanchions and barriers blocking flat surfaces and roadblocks on the streets accessing the hotel. This was no small task in that, even though the number of guests was greatly reduced to the Kissinger party and our group, the King David remained fully staffed and needed to function as a hotel, so workers were required to have identity cards at all times.

Police officers diverted traffic into a detour. Ropes and barricades kept crowds of fans and the merely curious several hundred feet away. Many of these devoted people held signs welcoming Taylor (fewer for Burton) and not a few held out single roses which they had heard was her favorite flower. (Supposedly it was actually sandalwood.) One woman kept stopping anybody who appeared to be in authority to tell them, "Everybody says I look like Elizabeth Taylor. Don't you think I look like Elizabeth Taylor?" Dark, with dark hair and too much eye makeup, she carried a photograph of herself that, perhaps on a full moon during a lightning storm, might have shown a slight resemblance. At least she was polite.

This was my first exposure to fandom. In fact, the word *fandom* hadn't even been invented at the time, it was just *fans*. Lots of them. *Fan* is short for *fanatic*, and there was no short supply of fanaticism on tap as the crowds parted for cars to drive in and out. From our first arrival I wondered why Burton and Taylor did not acknowledge the onlookers. Certainly a politician would have. But the celebrity couple knew something that I did not, which is that stars exist on the big screen, not in real life, and that the chasm between fantasy and reality is not only what makes the movies "the movies," it's what protects the people who become famous by appearing in them. The last thing Taylor or Burton wanted to do was start a riot despite the affection they felt flowing from the crowds. Their lack of attention wasn't arrogance, it was self-preservation.

The photographers were another matter. If they didn't sell a picture, they didn't eat. Popularized—or at least named—by Federico Fellini in his 1960 film *La Dolce Vita*, the paparazzi are independent photojournalists, not staffers, so every click missed is another lira or kopek lost. Famed for running after celebrities and chasing them in cars, they were not yet the desperate breed who would purposely provoke a fight or lob insults just to get a picture of the incensed star. In any event, Burton and Taylor were having none of it.

I returned half an hour later with the vodka and nodded my way through security, riding my Vespa right past the crowds without being recognized. When I got to the suite I knocked softly on Taylor's bedroom door.

"Who is it?" she said from inside.

"It's Yoram."

"Who?"

"Benny."

"Oh, okay. Would you leave it at the door?"

"You want some ice or tonic water or anything?"

"Why?" she asked. I left the bottle in a brown paper bag outside her bedroom door.

"See you at ten, right, Miss Taylor?" I asked in a hopeful manner. "Remember now: Masada?"

"Masada," she said through the door. It was about 8 A.M.

I went right away to our production office downstairs and found Dieter already poring through the morning papers looking for coverage. There was no shortage of it, but it did not make him happy.

"Where have you been?" he asked when I entered the office.

"I had an errand to run," I said, my discretion filter working.

"Look at these," he said, not caring what I'd just said. "Liz and Dick are the number one story. *Time* magazine. *Jerusalem Post*. *Ha'aritz*, The Associated Press. They're news everywhere."

"You must be thrilled," I said.

"It's a disaster," Dieter said. "They are the number one story. My film is not."

"Nowhere?"

"Not even a mention in passing. The only people getting any benefit from spending my money are two people who don't need it!"

"I wish I knew what to say," I said weakly.

"When are we getting together with Burton? We need to talk to him. He's the one who can make plans with us for the film."

"I don't know," I said. "He hasn't mentioned it to me either."

"Well then, we must make him remember that this is why he is here. Not to romance her, but to help us. Remember, it was he who wanted us to bring him here. She is merely along for the ride."

I had no answer.

Dieter closed the last of the papers and wiped his ink-smudged hands on a hotel towel. "*Scheisse!*"

At ten A.M., as promised, I knocked on Taylor's door. When there was no answer, I knocked again, louder. Perhaps she suspected that I would be there to awaken her, because at some time between my leaving her and this moment, she had unlocked it.

"Miss Taylor?" I said cautiously as I entered. "Are you all right?"

She made no sound. The shades had been pulled so I could not see whether her blankets were moving as she breathed. All I needed was for Elizabeth Taylor to die on my watch. Louder, I said, "Miss Taylor?"

She snored and rolled over. Then I saw the vodka bottle beside her bed. The bottle was empty. It couldn't have been more than two hours since I'd delivered it.

"*L'chaim*," I risked saying.

"*L'chaim*," she answered groggily.

"Miss Taylor, time to wake up."

"What time is it?"

"It's time to fly to Masada."

"In a plane?"

"We have to be at the airport at eleven. It's ten now. How soon can you be ready?"

"How about Passover?"

"Masada, Miss Taylor. What about the thousand Hebrews?"

"I'll drink to them."

"Looks like you already have."

She sighed and coughed. "I didn't ask to be famous."

"The public loves you."

"All I owe the public is my work, not my life," she said, and tried to go back to sleep.

"Please don't go back to sleep, Miss Taylor. Even if you don't go to Masada, you have things to do. We have to talk about the movie."

"Look, I'm not ungrateful," she said. At first I thought she was talking about Dieter and me bringing her and Burton to Israel, but no. "God knows it's made us rich, Richard and me. And if my fame can raise money for charity or bring attention to something worthwhile, then I'll use it. But that's not how it goes. Usually it's telephoto lenses shooting onto our yacht. Or it's a camera shoved under a lavatory stall. Can you imagine that? And then yesterday. I thought I was going to suffocate. I thought they were going to maul poor Nancy and me. People think we like the attention. We don't. Pray you're never famous."

I let her words settle. "What can I do for you, Miss Taylor," I finally asked.

"Let me go back to sleep."

I did.

At eleven o'clock at Atorot Airport, standing beside a rented single-engine Cessna, Nathan Goldstein checked his watch and started pacing. Half an hour later, still pacing, he checked the time again and sighed, "This is Yoram's revenge," before telling the pilot, "might as well put it back in the hangar."

* * *

While Taylor was resting, Burton was out on his own exploring the city. He had had the decency to leave me a note saying that, as long as he was in Jerusalem, he was going to the National Library to do some reading. He promised to return by afternoon. I hurried to our production office to tell Dieter that it might be opportune to corral him when he got back but, when I entered, I found myself being introduced to Gunter Schmidt.

"This is our partner," Dieter said as Schmidt and I shook hands. "He's from the German Cinema Investment Group. They're the financing entity for *Vergeltung*."

"You've come at the right time," I said, indicating the tearsheets that Dieter had tacked around the walls of the office. "Look, we're the lead story."

"*Jah?*" Schmidt said. "So what?"

"What do you mean so what?" I said using my best salesman manner. "This is great. Liz and Dick are the number one story everywhere."

"Correction," he snorted. "It is all Liz and Dick and their marriage plans. Blah blah blah. Not one word about our movie."

"One will lead to the other."

"Not soon enough."

I looked at Dieter who was sharing Schmidt's concern. "I don't understand what's going on here."

"Let me explain," Dieter said. "Have a seat." I did. "Herr Schmidt is the money, He came to bring us more."

"Not so fast," Schmidt countered. "I made some calls first. Do you know who you are dealing with?"

"You?" I ventured.

"*Them!*" he practically spat. "Do you know what they are called everywhere, except, apparently, between the two of you? They are called a lobby attraction. Do you know what a lobby attraction is? A lobby attraction is a celebrity that draws crowds when they walk into a hotel lobby, but then nobody buys tickets to see their motion pictures. And guess what. You have not one lobby attraction set to appear in our movie, but two of them."

"We need them to talk up *Vergeltung*," Dieter said firmly. "No more beating around the bush. They are here to sell the film. What about Taylor? Will she talk about it when she goes on tour today?"

"She's not going on tour," I said. "Yesterday scared the hell out of her and she said she's not going to leave the hotel any more."

"What about the other one?" Schmidt asked.

"Burton is at the library reading about Israel," I said.

"Very good, gentlemen," Schmidt said sarcastically. "You have one sleeper, one scholar, and no publicity. And now you don't even have your lobby attractions."

* * *

Depressed and feeling useless, I decided to go to Tel-Aviv. Perhaps Ani and Dory would lift my spirits.

When I stepped into our apartment the smell of flowers hit me full-on. "They're beautiful," Ani said from the kitchen where she was changing Dory. "And the boy who delivered them said they were from Richard Burton."

"It was a team effort," I hemmed.

"Speaking of a team effort," Ani said, "let me teach you how to diaper a baby."

She walked me through the powdering and positioning, but when it came to pinning the diaper on this tiny creature, I balked.

"I'm afraid I'll stick him," I said.

"Nonsense," she said. "I'll be watching you. Anyway, you're good at taking care of babies."

"Big babies. Actors."

"Is she really that beautiful?"

"She's that beautiful," I said. "Even in the morning without makeup."

"*In the morning?*" Ani said. I was afraid she'd stick the diaper pin on me.

"I think I've got it."

"No, I'll do it." She finished and held Dory in her arms. "See? All changed and ready to feed so we can change him again. What's Burton like?"

"There could be a mensch hiding in him somewhere," I said. "He's spending today at the library."

"Who's minding the store?"

"I am, in theory," I said, "although we seem to have a silent partner who hasn't been very silent lately."

"What do you mean?"

"Dieter has an investor from Munich who seems to be more than just an investor. I don't know how many strings he holds, but he's not averse to pulling them."

"Be careful," Ani said. "Don't sign anything."

"I won't," I assured her. "So far nothing's amiss, but I'll keep my eyes and ears open."

"Watch yourself," Ani said. She always had a sixth sense about people. I stayed a little while longer to watch her breast feed Dory. It was a gift seeing both of them so close and so much at peace. I was sorry I could not be with them every minute of every day.

* * *

That night I returned to the hotel to catch up on paperwork in the suite instead of risking another encounter with Schmidt in the production office. I hadn't realized that the sun had set until Burton entered wearing a hat and scarf despite the warm weather.

"What are you working on?" he asked solicitously.

"Budgets," I answered. "I'm trying to cut out the fat now that we have two of the world's greatest stars to carry instead of just one."

"By the time you start, Elizabeth and I will be sharing a room, if that helps," he smiled. I was charmed. He actually seemed looser without people around. He also carried a book.

"What are you reading?" I asked.

"*A History of the Jews in the Modern World* by Abram Sachar," he said, handing me the volume. "It's more recent than Biblical, but, I thought, 'When in Rome,' so to speak, although that's pathetically wrong for here, isn't it? After yesterday, I thought I'd see a bit of Jerusalem from the sidewalk instead of the street."

"Weren't you recognized? After all, you've been on every front page in town for the last two days."

"Let me tell you a secret, Benny: One is only recognized in public if one wants to be."

I looked at his disguise. "I'm sure the hat and scarf helped. It must look a little strange for late August. Where did you go?"

"Just walking around. I read some of my book, then walked a little more." He weighed the volume before setting it down. "I always thought that we Welsh were oppressed, but I see we have nothing compared to your people." He walked past me and stood before the large window facing the Old City. "Look how beautiful the Tower of David is."

I turned to look at what he was seeing. Caressed by floodlights, the majestic stone tower rose above the Old City. Two hundred feet away was the Jaffa Gate. It was a timeless tableaux and it gave me an adventurous idea.

"Let us wait another hour or two until the stores are closed and the streets are empty," I said, tantalizingly. "Then I will show you something very old in a way you have never seen it." I returned to my paperwork while Burton settled in with his book. I wanted so much to talk to him, learn about his life and experiences, but I could tell that he was relaxed for the first time since arriving in Israel, and I didn't want to break that spell.

At midnight we left stealthily out the back of the hotel, nodded discretely to the guards, and walked the five hundred meters on the dark dirt road leading through the Jaffa Gate into the Old City and the Tower of David. Burton seemed overcome by the vastness of it. I led him inside the building. He spun himself around, caught in its power, and steadied himself on a stone divider

"Are you all right?" I asked. He made no answer. "Over the centuries," I began, "this has changed hands dozens—scores—of times. It has been possessed and defiled by the Romans, the Ottomans, the Muslims, and the Crusaders. Finally it was restored by the Jews. It's still here, and so are we."

Burton stared strangely at me. "Before you were a producer, did you drive a tour bus?"

"No," I chuckled. "Every kid in Israel knows about this place."

It was past midnight. The pushcarts and tourists had gone and the area had become home to the people of the night. Arabs, Jews, a few stalwart tourists, dogs, goats, camels, and stragglers mixed informally and peacefully.

The lights illuminating the Tower contrasted with the shadows surrounding it. Burton went to one of the Jerusalem Stones that define the base of the Tower. His gaze became distant and his rich voice took on a mysterious tone.

"I am not a spiritual man," he began, "but I feel that I have been here before. These stones have seen many armies, have they not? My birthplace, Wales, has also suffered the unwelcome: the Romans, the Barbarians, the Celts. Like you, we survived, although at times our culture was buried." He led me farther toward the stony base of the Tower. "The Tower of David draws its name from King Solomon's *Song of Songs*, does it not?"

Before I could say Yes, Burton knelt on the soiled stones and lay flat on his stomach, extending his arms outward, reaching out and touching and squeezing the dirt with his hands.

"What are you doing?" I asked, bending down to help him get up. He pushed my hand away.

"I kneel at the altar of history," he said, his voice seemingly elsewhere. "I lie prostrate in the presence of holiness."

I looked around. Fortunately, no one was noticing. He got up and stood facing the Tower, not even trying to brush the dust and grime from his expensive clothes. I stood close to see if he had been drinking. There was no smell of alcohol on his breath, and his burning eyes were as clear as the sky as he recited, from memory, the *Song of Solomon*.

"This is for you, Elizabeth," he whispered, then continued, "Behold, thou art fair, my love; behold, thou art fair; thou hast doves' eyes within thy locks. Thy lips are like a thread of scarlet, and thy speech is comely: thy temples are like a piece of a pomegranate within thy locks. Thy neck is like the Tower of David builded for an armoury, whereon there hang a thousand bucklers, all shields of mighty men. Thy two breasts are like two young roes that are twins, which feed among the lilies. Until the day break, and the shadows flee away, I will get me to the mountain of myrrh, and to the hill of frankincense. Thou art all fair, my love; there is no spot in thee."

The mere reading of those sacred words surprised me. They are moving to anyone who appreciates their poetry and their history, but when a gifted actor like Richard Burton recites them from his heart, they become hypnotic. His speaking drew the attention of people in the plaza. They came alive, looked to him, and were energized by the power and passion behind his voice.

Only when he finished did he notice how soiled he was.

"It's only dirt," he said dismissively, when I helped him up and pointed to the stains. "In Pontrhydyfen, where I was born, dirt from the mines covered everything—our faces, our clothes, our souls, our dreams. My father was a coal miner; it covered him, too. It is dirt from which I must be reborn." He brushed the soil from his clothing. "Sometimes you need to climb again from dirt. Elizabeth, too. Our love and our careers will be reborn together here. This is why I am doing your film. I need it to put my feet back on the ground."

I didn't know what to say. How had he been moved to such an extent by a screenplay with the unlikely name of *Vergeltung*? "The script means that much to you?" I asked.

He looked at me suspiciously. "Have you read it?" I kept diplomatically silent. He understood. "Let me tell you something," he whispered. "At this point I would do anything to save my career."

I had to press. "All right, then," I said, "but what about the stage?"

"I haven't been before a live audience in more than ten years."

"But what about Mayor Kollek's invitation . . . ?"

"Impossible. But I didn't want to disappoint him in front of the others."

This I could not accept. Forgetting that he was famous, I spoke to him as a father would speak to a child who gave up at sports after showing his prowess. "I can't accept this, Mr. Burton. You just gave a brilliant performance of the Song of Solomon. How many other things have you memorized?"

Burton did not choose to argue. "No." His mind was fixed.

So was mine. "These people here, all around us, they didn't know you were famous and yet you mesmerized them. They didn't understand your language and yet you held them in the palm of your hand. Please, Mr. Burton. Whatever happens to you in film, you are a creature of the live stage. Don't deny us that."

He paused. At first I thought he was considering my logic. Then he said something that transcended logic and spoke to my heart.

"I think it's time you called me Richard."

We looked around. In the heat of his performance we hadn't considered that he was doing something unexpected and that strangers would notice. People were approaching warily, perhaps starting to recognize him, which meant that we had to leave, and quickly, lest there be another scene.

"All right, then, please *Richard*. Come along," I urged.

As we walked along, his mood lightened. "But you must never call me 'Dick' just as you must never call Elizabeth 'Liz.' That is reserved for the tabloids—and for us when we fight. We detest 'Liz and Dick.'"

We walked a few more steps and then I stopped.

"What is it?" Richard said.

"I am calling your bluff. Perform at the Jerusalem Theatre. We both know you can do it."

"It cannot happen."

I can twist the knife too. "I can't believe that you, of all people, lack courage."

That started the gears turning in his magnificent brain. He stared at me and I stared back. Then he said, "No promises, but when is the performance?"

"The sabbath comes out about 8 o'clock. The performance should begin by 8:30."

There was a long pause as we kept walking. Finally he said, "If I agreed—I say *if*—when could we check out the theatre?"

"Friday before Sabbath starts. What would you need?"

He recited a checklist. "Lighting? Props? Acoustics? All I need is an armchair and a carafe of water. And make sure Elizabeth is sitting in front."

Why not push it? "What will you perform?"

"Whatever comes into my head."

"I'll call Mayor Kollek before you change your mind."

We walked a little farther and then Richard turned and leaned into my face. "You are one tenacious bastard. But, then, you want to be a producer, don't you?"

He walked on. I stopped and called to him. "What made you say yes?"

"Your remark about courage."

We walked another fifty feet in silence. Then I said, "Richard?"

"What?"

"If you want to see real courage, you and Miss Taylor should come with me tomorrow and meet an eight-day-old baby with a lot of it."

He wasn't sure what I was talking about but, by now, he seemed to trust me. And a good thing it turned out to be.

9

THE NARROW STREET IN FRONT of Ani's and my apartment building in Tel Aviv was blocked by the limousine I had arranged to bring our two famous guests to Dory's bris. More widely known as a circumcision, the removal of a male child's penile foreskin eight days after his birth is a covenant told in Genesis between God and the Jews. Circumcision has been performed by Semitic people and others for thousands of years. It is not a universal practice; many cultures avoid it and there are those who consider it to be mutilation. Within Judaism, however, it is a joyous event (well, except for the circumcisee) that welcomes a new member, so to speak, into the community.

It was this celebration to which I had invited Richard Burton and Elizabeth Taylor. To my astonishment, they accepted. I did not tell Dieter, whom I also asked to come, in case they were a no-show, and he was astonished when he saw them enter our tiny apartment.

Taylor arrived with her head covered respectfully in a scarf and kissed her fingers, pressing them to the mezuzah on our doorframe. Burton took her cue and did the same, then accepted a yarmulke from a man who handed it to him as he stepped inside. One by one our guests recognized the famous couple and the room fell uncomfortably silent. I decided it was my job to break the ice. "*Shalom!*" I said. Taylor responded with "*Shalom!*" and the room came back to life as she and Burton introduced themselves to those around them.

I led them to Ani and Dory. "This is Ani," I said, "and this is Dory."

Both Taylor and Burton said "*Shalom.*"

Ani said, "*Shalom*" and continued in English, proudly holding up Dory for Taylor to inspect. The actress carefully unwrapped the blankets from our son's face and stroked his forehead with her hand, offering the traditional greeting, "Welcome to the world. May you be blessed." Then she returned him to his mother.

Ani handed Dory to the sandek, who happened to be my father, who held him on his lap in preparation for the ritual. The mohel, who would perform the circumcision, dipped the corner of a clean handkerchief into sweet kosher wine and put it in Dory's mouth. The boy immediately sucked on it and the tiny amount of alcohol went to work. This is done to help the infant relax and dull the pain, but no one really knows if it does any good. In theory the child gets over the pain, although from time to time the tradition causes controversy.

The alcohol having gone to work, the mohel cleared his throat to gain the floor. Men who had been praying knew it was his turn to speak. The mohel took two knives from a box: his own *brit milah* blade and a second one that he handed to me. This would make me his proxy in the way that Abraham circumcised his son, Isaac, in the Old Testament.

"Blessed are you Hashem," the mohel began, "King of the universe, Who has sanctified us with His commandments and commanded us regarding circumcision."

He handed me a card from which I read, "Blessed are you Hashem, King of the universe, Who has sanctified us with His commandments and commanded us to enter Dory Ben-Ami into the Covenant of Abraham our father." (Abraham is regarded as the first modern Jew.)

The room held its breath while the mohel made a swift, clean cut. The only sound was Dory who let out a tiny scream. It was immediately drowned by fifty people shouting, "Mazel Tov!" All except Dieter who whispered, "This is barbaric."

Burton heard this and teased him smilingly, "This, coming from a German?"

Lifting Dory and handing him to Ani, the mohel proclaimed, "One day this little one will be a big one!"

Whispered Burton to Taylor, "Not if they keep cutting it off."

Taylor could give it as well as take it. "You know, Richard, if you really want to become Jewish, now's your chance."

Burton stepped forward to shake my hand and kiss Ani on the cheek. Meanwhile, Taylor took the mohel aside. "Excuse me, rabbi."

"Thank you, but I am not a rabbi," he said, "I am a mohel. You might say I'm a specialist."

"You were so gentle, I wonder if you also do weddings."

"Again, Miss Taylor," he said, "that's for a rabbi. Any rabbi in Israel can do a marriage. Who's getting married?"

"Mr. Burton and me."

The mohel furrowed his brow. "Where do you intend this to take place?"

"Right here in the Holy Land," she said proudly.

The mohel shook his head. "I'm afraid that's impossible."

"Why?" she asked. "We're both single."

"No, no, you don't understand," he said, drawing her aside for privacy. "You are a Jew. He is not. There is no rabbi in all Israel who will marry a Jew to a non-Jew."

"What if he converts?"

"You yourself know what that involves. I am sorry. I cannot help you. Please excuse me."

He left a stunned Taylor and returned to check on Dory's bleeding and to pack his equipment.

Taylor looked across the room at Burton who was enjoying hobnobbing with the others. He looked relaxed. She would break the bad news to him later and wonder whether he would change his mind about the marriage. She had not changed hers.

* * *

Dieter finished his fourth schnapps. Schmidt had had none. The two men were closing down a small restaurant and discussing finances.

"Dieter, my friend," Schmidt said, "It is time, as they say in the movie business, to shit or get off the pot."

"I know," Dieter said.

"You have been listening too much to this Israeli who says wait, wait, wait."

"I know."

"You have been spending my money all week and for what? A wedding announcement for two faded movie stars? A tour of the city that helped everyone but us?"

"I know." He was becoming more dejected with each acknowledgment.

"There is only one way for you to save our project, my investment, and yourself. You must have these movie people make a public announcement and commit to making the film. Only then will there be any chance of full financing. Perhaps there are some investors who still believe that old Hollywood exists and will commit to the money."

"I know."

"You need a plan, Dieter. You need it now."

"I know," Dieter said. "You gave me an idea."

That night, still feeling the effects of the schnapps, Dieter wrote a letter, sealed it, and navigated his way down the corridor of the King David Hotel to the Burton-Taylor Suite. Sidestepping the floral arrangements that were still arriving on a daily basis, he slid the letter under the door of Burton's bedroom and returned to his hotel room to sleep it off.

* * *

Friday morning I was folding my linens and stowing the sofa bed when Burton entered from his bedroom holding a letter. He didn't tell me what it was but he spoke sharply to me. "Go fetch Dieter Kraus."

"Is something wrong?" I asked.

Burton spoke as if issuing a proclamation: "Go. Fetch. Dieter. Kraus."

I foolishly misinterpreted his mood and rushed to the *Vergeltung* production office where Dieter was looking through equipment rental manuals.

"Grab the script," I said excitedly. "He wants to talk about our project."

Dieter brightened. "It worked."

"What worked?" I said to his back as he beat me out the door.

Dieter got to the suite first where Burton was waiting. I followed. Burton was grim. He held up his hand to stop Dieter near the door. I froze, too.

Burton held up the letter as if he had just lifted it from the toilet. "Is this your letter to me? Did you write this?"

"Yes," Dieter said proudly.

"And slip it under my door in the dead of night?"

"Yes I did."

"What kind of rubbish is this letter?" he went on, using his stage voice to make his point. "You are accusing Elizabeth and me of not being interested in your project, of not cooperating in publicizing it." He scanned the letter to find the place he wanted to read. "'While you have not had time to discuss *Vergeltung*, Miss Taylor has somehow made herself available to go sightseeing, dine with Henry Kissinger, miss an appointment with the Film Minister, and do all her Jewish stuff.'" He looked daggers at Dieter. "'Jewish stuff' coming from a German?"

I must admit that I flinched at hearing "all her Jewish stuff." Even though Dieter was German, he had never given so much as a hint of prejudice.

Burton continued reading the letter with a voice that could have performed an exorcism: "'I brought you here at your request at great expense to me. Now I must demand that you and Miss Taylor make a public announcement that you intend to star in my film.'"

Dieter froze in his place. His face grew red. Burton looked up from the letter and spoke to Dieter as if I were not standing in the same room.

"You are a monumentally foolish and supremely stupid man. This letter is your resignation from the motion picture business. I could take this letter and sue you for a million dollars. 'All her Jewish stuff?' How dare you! If you ever decide to write a letter like this again, make sure you show it to your lawyer first and let him tell you how dangerously ignorant you are."

Dieter didn't know where to look or what to do with himself, so he stood in his place and took it.

"Fraud, defamation, breach of implied contract," Burton continued, "need I go on? If you're smart, which I doubt, you'll leave this room, which you must, leave this country, which you shall, and leave this business, which you should. Now go. *Schnell!*"

I could see Dieter trying to think of something to say, or even some way to charm his way out of this, but he was coming up dry. Wisely, he chose to leave the suite. I began to follow him when Burton said, "Where are you going, Yoram?"

I faced Burton. He laid the letter aside and immediately relaxed.

"Do you want a drink?" he said.

"Um, no," I stammered.

Ignoring me, he said, "Help yourself" and pointed to the small refrigerator. "I could use a club soda." I opened the door and the appliance was still stocked with juices, sodas, healthful snacks, and no liquor. "Out of the bottle is fine." I found an opener and brought each of us a club soda. "Cheers," Burton said, and we clinked bottles.

After draining his small bottle and suppressing a belch, he looked at me and said, "You're not off the hook yet, either."

I set my bottle down.

"Tell me straight," he went on, "Just between us, did the State of Israel really invite Elizabeth and me?"

"No," I blushed. "I sent you the invitation myself."

"Is the Israeli government paying for any of this?"

"No," I confessed. "Dieter is paying for it. But he really does want to make the film with you."

Burton became grim again. "There will be no film. But you know this by now, don't you."

I nodded in acknowledgment. He had me dead to rights. "And it's too bad," I said. "This country needs to make films with stars like you. You and Miss Taylor could have made that happen."

Burton finished his soda. "Can you find out how much this little gambit has cost Herr Kraus?"

"I can tell you now because I am keeping the books. He had fifty thousand. So far we owe sixty-two thousand, five hundred dollars and I have no idea where we'll find it."

To my surprise, Burton didn't even pause for a second. He reached behind his chair and lifted his book bag from the floor. He took out his checkbook and started writing. I remember thinking what it must be like to write a check of any size and not have to look at the register to see if there were enough funds to cover it.

"Here," he said, handing me the check. "Sixty-two thousand, five hundred dollars. Give this to Kraus, tell him we're even, and tell him never to speak to either Elizabeth or me again."

"You're very kind," I managed to say.

"No, it's just that I've discovered that money is the always cheapest way to pay for anything."

I tucked the check in my shirt pocket. I was stunned, not just at his generosity, but by the fact that he knew not only that we had been using the two of them but that he seemed to hint that they had been using us. Burton said, "One more thing. Get us out of here tomorrow morning back to Switzerland, would you?" Then he added, "Please."

"It's Friday," I said. "There'll be no planes out until Saturday night. It's Sabbath." I began to leave, then remembered. "Besides, what about the children?"

Burton looked confused. "What children?"

"Your performance. The one tomorrow night at the Jerusalem Theatre so children can see plays. They've been selling tickets."

"Then they'd better start giving refunds."

"But Mr. Burton—Richard—you can't. You're the world's greatest living stage actor. You can't deny them the chance to see you."

"I've just bailed you out with a check for sixty-two thousand dollars. How much chutzpah do you have?"

"Enough to ask you to keep your word—for the sake of the children."

"I can't perform."

"But the Tower of David!" I was almost frantic. "You knew the Song of Solomon by heart! I've seen you on chat shows. You've got half of Shakespeare and God knows what else in your brain. Surely you can summon it for charity. You can't change your mind." I studied his face. He studied mine. When he dropped his gaze, I knew he was on the fence and just needed a slight push to do what he secretly wanted to do anyway.

"If you can't be in our film," I said gently, "at least be on our stage. After all," I said, teasing him, "the State of Israel welcomes you."

He laughed heartily and told me to confirm with the theatre. I shook his hand and left his suite feeling proud, but also angry at Dieter.

I tried to contain my temper as I walked through the flower-riddled corridors and stormed into the production office.

"What were you thinking?" I began my harangue. "You couldn't wait? Why didn't you at least warn me you were going to sneak a letter under his door? Why not a lit fuse?"

"They were just wasting our time and money," Dieter maintained.

"Your time and my money! You know that."

"I agreed to work on spec because I hoped you wouldn't be a fool. Now you've made me one."

"They made fools of both of us."

"We almost had them!"

Dieter folded his arms and laughed. "Do not delude yourself. They had us. A free trip? The King David Hotel? A tour of the city? Brushing shoulders with politicians and diplomats? Some day I would like to have an all-expense paid vacation like this one!"

At this point I reached into my shirt pocket and handed him Burton's check.

"What is this?"

"Richard Burton's personal check for everything you spent. Sixty-two thousand, five hundred dollars. All expenses paid back. He doesn't owe us anything."

"It isn't enough," he said, putting the check in his own pocket.

"What are you talking about?" I said. "It's every penny we spent. I kept the books."

"I am sure he will change his mind when I complete the financing and tell him that the film is set to roll."

"That's your problem," I said, marveling that he refused to give up.

And indeed he didn't give up. Dieter ran with the project for the next twenty years, never quite finding the money, never losing hope, always thinking that somehow he was going to make the movie. "As for me," I said, heading toward the door, "I am going home to my wife and son. I'll see you tomorrow night at the theatre."

10

FRIDAY AFTERNOON, BURTON AND I slipped away to visit the Jerusalem Theatre so he could check out the facilities. The theatre proudly informed us that tickets at 100 Israeli pounds were already moving faster than expected and that they anticipated a full house for Saturday night. Shabbat was due to end just before 8 P.M. and they had called curtain time for 8:30. That didn't give much time to set up the stage—nobody could touch lights or do any kind of work during Sabbath—so they were pleased when Burton said he wanted only a chair and general lighting. And he made sure that they would hold two seats in the front row for Taylor and her friend, the hairdresser.

When we got back to the hotel I returned a call from Shimon Peres's office to confirm the arrangements for that night's Sabbath dinner at his and his wife Sonia's home. Originally, all of us had been invited. Now his secretary was saying that Peres wanted a more intimate dinner and so only Taylor and Burton were asked to attend. The invitation no longer included Dieter and me.

This outraged me. Whatever else, Dieter and I were the ones who had brought Taylor and Burton to Israel. We were not their social directors, we were trying to get a film made. I guess I was finally succumbing to the same impatience that was driving Dieter to distraction. Even if we knew that the film would not happen, others didn't, and so it was time for me to act like a producer and throw my weight around. Everyone else in town seemed to be profiting from Burton and Taylor's visit, why not me?

"Miss Taylor and Mr. Burton will not be able to attend dinner," I firmly told Peres's secretary, "unless Mr. Kraus and I are also invited."

"I'm not sure that those arrangements can be made on such short notice," the secretary said.

"Fine," I told her, probably speaking louder than I should, "then you will have two empty seats at the table and you can fill them with anybody you like."

There was an uncomfortable pause and the sound of a hand being placed over the receiver. I could hear muffled mumbling through it.

"All right, Mr. Ben-Ami, we will be glad to have you. Shabbat comes in at 6:33. Mrs. Peres will light candles before that. I'll leave your names with the security people. *Shabbat shalom.*"

Leaving Burton at the hotel, I returned to Ani's and my apartment in Tel Aviv. Dory's circumcision was healing properly and he had no trouble using his bulbul to flood diaper after diaper. Ani and I folded them from the wash tub.

"I'm sorry I let you down," I said. "I really thought this film had a chance of going. I'm sure I'll find another job soon. A real one."

"What happened to the young man who talked his way into a job with Otto Preminger?" she asked.

"You did."

"I wouldn't worry," Ani said. "I'm sure Burton and Taylor won't have any problem finding work now that they've gotten all this publicity." She paused. "What's going to happen with Dieter?"

I shrugged.

"I'll just ask this once," she said, looking up from her folding. "Did you sign anything? Did you commit to anything?"

"No."

"Then what do you think will happen?"

"I don't know. All I know is, all I have left to do is deliver Burton to the theatre on Saturday night."

"Dieter and his money, Burton and stage fright. Liz the lush. You ought to find a safer line of work—like clearing land mines."

I laughed. "Some day this'll make a great movie," I agreed. "Whatever happens, I have you and Dory."

"And about twenty diapers you still have to fold."

Ani left to check on Dory and, standing there taking care of my share of the laundry, it struck me that cleaning up his children's poo is what a young producer really does well.

* * *

Although he would later serve several terms as Israel's President as well as other offices (Prime Minister, Minister of Foreign Affairs), at this time Shimon Peres was Minister of Defense, having succeeded our national war hero Moshe Dayan (the general with the eyepatch). Shimon and Sonia Peres lived in a spacious, art-filled penthouse at Oppenheimer 12 in Ramat Aviv, a suburb of Tel Aviv. Whether they were aware that I had forced Dieter and myself on them, I don't know, but they were both gracious hosts in the centuries-old tradition of inviting travelers to join Sabbath dinner.

As instructed by the religion, the women covered their heads and Mrs. Peres lit two candles to keep the Sabbath. After the Defense Minister intoned the traditional blessing, he passed around the Kiddush cup of wine for everyone to take a sip. When it came Burton's turn, he discretely handed it, like a good little boy, to Elizabeth without partaking. It was interesting to watch Taylor, who knew the ritual, coach Burton in the process. It was even more interesting to watch poor Dieter—seated as far away from Burton as possible but still uncomfortable

Observant enough to follow Sabbath tradition but secular enough to have servants bring food to the table, the Pereses welcomed all of us to their home. It was hard to think of any moment in Israel's history of which Shimon Peres was not a part. A protégé of founder David Ben-Gurion, he was a poet, scholar, extraordinary speaker, and a master of at least six languages (although some say that, when he spoke Hebrew, he betrayed his Polish roots).

Unlike her charismatic and engaging husband, Sonia Gelman Peres was exceptionally private and preferred to work with sick and disabled children and dodge the spotlight as much as Shimon craved it. They were an unusual couple (and, in fact, would split in 2007 when she famously refused to move with him from Tel Aviv to Jerusalem when he was elected to the Israeli Presidential residence. They would divorce in 2011).

"It has been impossible not to know that you have come to Israel to make a motion picture," Peres said to Burton and Taylor. "What can you tell us about it? Is it a romance? A spectacle?"

Rather than be forced to lie, Burton deferred to Dieter, saying, "Why don't you answer that, Mr. Kraus. After all, it's your film."

Dieter looked surprised. After all, hadn't Burton just read him the riot act? Now he was moved by Burton's gesture to make peace with him and eagerly took up the challenge. "It has some of everything," he said. "It's a love story, it has action, it shows off a young country, it shows the life of immigrants, everything. Everything," he smiled proudly, "except politics."

"That is good to know," Peres said as if making a speech. "Israel needs foreign movies to be filmed in Israel. It helps our economy and it helps to train our crews and actors. I appreciate that you came here."

The dinner moved on from there. Dieter and I made polite chatter with those around us but we knew that nobody was there to speak with us. After dinner, as Mrs. Peres supervised clearing the table, her husband, Burton, and Taylor continued their conversation, walking through the large living room and stepping out onto the penthouse balcony. Dieter and I followed, hanging back to give them privacy while still being able to witness three world-famous people relax with each other.

Peres leaned forward, resting his forearms on the balcony railing. Looking out over the beautiful city of Tel Aviv on this warm August night—its roads glowing gold from streetlamps and thousands of homes twinkling with Sabbath candles—and seeing Shimon Peres, who had so much to do with making it possible—was extremely moving.

Burton and Taylor joined him on either side, all three staring out over the expanse of the city.

"Did you enjoy your dinner with Dr. Kissinger the other night?" Peres said. "If you don't mind, what did he tell you about his diplomatic plans here?"

"He was very—diplomatic," Taylor said, avoiding the question. "All he would say was that he felt optimistic that he could bring about peace. What do you think?"

Peres did not share the Secretary's optimism. "What else could he say? He must deal with Hafez al-Assad, and Hafez al-Assad is a stubborn man. He has consolidated his power as Syria's President, and there are none left who will question him. I'm not sure even Kissinger can persuade him of anything."

"Is there any hope, then, for the peace process?" Burton asked.

Peres thought for a moment and clearly did not want to render a judgment. "I wish him luck," he said instead. "We all need peace. It will be good for us and also for the Arab countries. As to how to achieve that peace. . . ." He let the sentence hang in the air.

"What part can the United States play?" Taylor pressed.

"Dr. Kissinger is a friend of Israel," Peres said, then smiled. "But he is also a friend of himself. As long as Israel's interests are the same as America's, our hopes and prayers travel in the same direction." At this point, Peres grew suddenly serious. "America can play the game of courtesy, but for Israel it is a matter of existing or not existing."

Burton did not miss the phrase. "You mean, 'to be or not to be.'"

"Yes," said Peres. "As we say in Hebrew, '*Leiot o lo leiot*.' To be or not to be."

"That *is* the question," said Burton, beginning Hamlet's soliloquy.

Then Peres picked it up in Hebrew. "Whether 'tis nobler in the mind to suffer the slings and arrows of outrageous fortune . . .'"

Burton accepted the challenge in English. "Or to take arms against a sea of troubles and, by opposing, end them."

The two men batted cues back and forth like a verbal tennis game—Burton in English and Peres in Hebrew—at times speaking over each other, each in his own language, until Peres had to yield to Burton's experience.

"Thus conscience does make cowards of us all," Burton concluded, "and thus the native hue of resolution is sicklied o'er with the pale cast of thought, and enterprises of great pitch and moment with this regard their currents turn awry and lose the name of action."

When he finished, Taylor said proudly, "Bravo! You do know that Richard's *Hamlet* on Broadway in 1964 was the most successful American run of all time. Do you know how it came about?" Peres did not. "Richard and Peter O'Toole had just finished working together and were drinking in a pub. At some point in the evening they both dared each other to play the Danish prince. But which of them would play it on Broadway and which in the West End? They settled it by flipping a coin. O'Toole got to stay in London and Richard lit up Broadway for one hundred and thirty-seven performances."

"Elizabeth is my best publicist," Burton said, and kissed her on the cheek.

"Is that what you'll be performing tomorrow night at the Jerusalem Theatre?" the Defense Minister asked.

"I'm not sure yet," Burton wavered. "A little Shakespeare, a little Dylan Thomas, a little scripture. Whatever comes to mind. I believe I should thank you for allowing me to rehearse in front of you just now."

"My pleasure," Peres said. "I wish I could attend, but I'm committed elsewhere. But you'll be there, won't you Miss Taylor?"

Taylor beamed at Burton as she told Peres, "I wouldn't miss it for all the ego in Hollywood. Thank you so much for this evening."

"Me too," Burton said. "Shabbat shalom."

11

THE NIGHT OF SATURDAY, AUGUST 30, after sabbath ended across Israel, was when the Jerusalem Theatre came alive. The front of the theatre sported a poster reading "Richard Burton Charity Performance tonight at 8:30" but it was just a formality as all 950 seats had been sold out within hours of the confirmation that the star would appear. When we did our Friday walk-through, Richard said he still didn't know what his selections were going to be. "I like to keep it loose," he said, but he and I both knew that he was still lining up his nerve.

Hailed for his stage work in Britain in the 1950s—he was called the successor to Laurence Olivier by critic Kenneth Tynan—Burton was born Richard Jenkins, Jr. in Pontrhydyfen, Wales, in 1925. The twelfth of thirteen children, he was raised by his sister, Cis, after their mother died when he was three. Never far from literature or his intense interest in rugby (he once said he'd rather play for Wales at Cardiff Arms Park than *Hamlet* at the Old Vic), he was taken under the wing of his schoolmaster, Philip Burton, when he was twelve. Burton shaped young Richard for the classics by helping him polish his voice and pronunciation. He also tried adopting the boy, but a legal snag prevented it; instead, Richard became Burton's ward and took his last name. He was given an internship at Exeter College and immediately drew attention for his acting skill and stage presence. Acting was interrupted by service in the RAF from 1943 to 1947, and after his discharge he began winning roles in British films as well as the interest of the nation's theatre royalty—John Gielgud, in particular. In 1949 he married Sybil Williams, a union that lasted until he met Taylor during the filming of *Cleopatra* in 1962. More films and less theatre followed (with the notable exceptions of the Broadway musical *Camelot* in 1960 and *Hamlet* in 1964) until Burton became known more for his screen work than for the electricity he generated on the boards.

Taking the live stage for the Jerusalem Theatre benefit performance would be, by any measure, a personal renaissance and a career resurrection. Not only was he returning to sobriety, he was returning to his roots, and, with both, would come self-respect.

As showtime arrived, the theatre filled with a human map of Israel. Young and old, Sephardem and Ashkenaz, Sabra and returned, resident and tourist, Jewish and gentile, and all variations that make up our nation. It made me think that, regardless of the uncertainties of the so-called "Peace Process," it is the arts that truly can unify us and bring peace.

Per Burton's instructions, the stage was set with only an easy chair and a small table on which was placed a drinking glass and, conspicuously, a carafe of water.

I waited in the dressing room with Burton, Taylor, and Jason while Mayor Kollek welcomed the audience to their applause. "Thank you ladies and gentlemen—and the children of Israel," he began. "I am pleased to report that every single ticket for this event sold out in one day. Hundred pound tickets were grabbed up in *one day!*" The people who had bought those tickets applauded themselves as well as the achievement. Kollek continued, "I am also pleased to report that the money raised by this event will enable the Jerusalem Theatre Fund to have every child see at least one live play here this year." More applause. It trailed into the green room where Burton was pacing.

"I was a fool to say yes to this," he said.

"No you weren't," Taylor assured him. "I'm here." She turned to Jason, who had not let the jewel case out of his possession, and said, "I think it's time for 'it.'"

Jason opened the case and handed the Cartier diamond to Burton who rose and fastened it lovingly around Taylor's neck. As he did, she told him softly, "You'll be wonderful, my dearest. You'll carry on stage with you the confidence of my love."

That done, Burton cracked open a fresh bottle of club soda and downed half of it. "Do you know," he said through a small belch, "in all my professional life I have never gone on stage without at least one drink in me."

It was only then that I cast my eyes past him to a full bar set up at the far end of the dressing room. It was there for the post-performance reception, but Taylor followed my gaze and then looked back at me. For an instant I thought I saw a flash of concern in her eyes, then it disappeared.

The Stage Manager, a young woman in her twenties, popped into the green room to say, "The Mayor is finishing, Mr. Burton. Follow me, please."

"I'll be along," he said. Then to us: "Give me a moment."

With that, Taylor and her makeup lady walked unnoticed to the seats in the front row that Burton had requested be held for them. On stage, Kollek was indeed finishing his introduction: "Very few people have the magic possessed by our guest. By both guests, actually. We spent some time together seeing the city and I cannot think of two more pleasant, considerate, generous companions. Now I should like to present the star of tonight's event, Mr. Richard Burton."

Hearing his name, Burton emerged deliberately from the dressing room and took center stage to loud applause. He shook the mayor's hand and said, "Thank you, Mayor Kollek," but few heard him in the overwhelming applause. He took a bow and waited for the house to settle. When the thunderous welcome persisted, he stood in place and enjoyed it.

Finally he began reciting the twenty-third psalm, only he did it in his native Welch, a language that had the audience looking at each other trying to determine what he was saying.

(NOTE: For the text of Burton's readings, please refer to the Appendix.)

Burton seemed to enjoy baffling the audience, but he had another trick up his sleeve.

"That was the twenty-third psalm in Welsh, my language," he said. "Now I shall try to do it in your language."

Hearing it in Hebrew, the audience at first gasped, then began wildly applauding, appreciating the gesture, as Burton continued—in Hebrew with a British accent. The audience immediately appreciated his reaching out to them with this grand gesture. When he concluded, Burton smiled broadly. He looked down at Taylor and winked. She winked back. He was off and running.

"Thank you," he said as the applause died. "I am so very grateful that you have come tonight and I appreciate your welcome.

"As we know, the Book of Samuel tells the history of King David and his powerful leadership. Today the world needs powerful leaders—powerful and just. Perhaps those we elect might look to the words of the

Prophets for guidance. This is David's lament over Saul and Jonathan." He recited the piece.

From the wings, I could see that Burton was once again back in his element. I watched Taylor gazing at him intently with such love flowing from her face that she must have been reminded of the the Burton that she knew from the days when their love lit up headlines all over the world.

On stage, Burton shifted the mood expertly. "Thank you, ladies and gentlemen. You're too kind. Now to Shakespeare, who wrote about another warrior king, Henry the Fifth, who led England into battle against France at Agincourt in the year 1415 during the Hundred Years War. With this speech, Henry rallied his troops, and it has the same power 400 years after William Shakespeare wrote it."

Burton then launched into the St. Crispin's day speech, the Shakespearean warhorse that rallies the troops into battle. Spoken with mounting passion and Burton's marvelous voice, the words seemed even more rousing spoken before an audience tempered by an ongoing war between young Israel and its neighbors.

Burton, out of breath from the rousing climax of Henry's speech, looked in amazement at his hypnotized audience. He smiled and began taking them into his confidence.

"When you play enough Shakespeare, you learn that the best roles to have are royalty. They don't always have the best lines, but they're the only ones who get to sit down now and then." The audience laughed politely at this insider's joke. Burton, who had been standing, sat in his easy chair. Then they got the joke.

"One of the kings I find it most satisfying to play is Richard the Second, because he gets to say the 'Hollow Crown' speech, one of the most philosophical in all of Shakespeare."

As with his Henry V speech, the Hollow Crown touched on the importance of leadership tempered by the weight of it.

Now fully comfortable once again on a stage in front of people, he stood and seemed to draw energy from the cosmos as he set up his next soliloquy. He spoke in tones so confident that he commanded attention. The audience hung on his every word.

"The best-known and most-performed of Shakespeare's plays is, of course, *Hamlet*. It has been called the story of a man who couldn't make up his mind. But I like to think it reflects the dilemma of seeking truth and finding, to the point of paralysis, how elusive the truth can be. In this soliloquy, Hamlet plots to expose the newly crowned king as the murderer of the old king, Hamlet's father, whom he dearly loved. He has enlisted the help of a troupe of players and is incensed that the actors can summon more emotion than he can."

He dipped his head, shook his arms as if to loosen them, and appeared to go into a trance. Becoming Hamlet, he sputtered self-loathing over his failure to avenge his dear father's death, then turned on a dime when he realiszed that he had the power in his hands to extract a confession from his uncle. The house fell silent as his manner drew them into his deadly conspiracy as Hamlet tricks the king into confessing.

Burton's reading was loud, soft, hostile, subtle, haunting and, by the end, determined. Once released from the grip of his taut attention, the house exploded in applause. Those who knew the speech had gasped at appropriate moments as he recited it, while others seemed to hold their breath till the end. It took a great deal out of him. He poured water from the carafe into his glass and started sipping it, pausing after one or two swallows to lift the glass for the audience's scrutiny.

"It's water," he said. The audience laughed. "Water reclaimed by Israel from the sea." He lowered his voice and said, almost as if only for himself, "Many things have been reclaimed here tonight."

Then it was back to business. "Dylan Thomas—like me, a Welshman—said of his play 'Under Milk Wood' that it is a play for voices. And if you let the voices run over you, they become a kind of music, describing the dreams of a Welsh fishing village that exists only in the mind of the writer."

As Thomas composed, Burton began "at the beginning" and described, in words that sounded like music, the village of the author's imagination. The piece—difficult enough for English speakers to grasp, let alone an audience in which many of whom knew English as a second language—was greeted with milder applause. He looked out at the audience warmly and then a sly smile appeared on his face as if he was keeping a secret. "Thank you, Ladies and Gentlemen," he said, enjoying their attention. "I know that you appreciate me, but I also know that I am not the one you really came here to see tonight." The audience got the clue and they began cheering and clapping. While they did, he walked down the stairs at the edge of the stage, stepped to the front row where Taylor was seated, and offered her his hand. She took it and rose, and, like a royal couple, they strode together up and across to center stage.

"May I introduce my fiancée, Miss Elizabeth Taylor."

The audience's ovation was overwhelming. Most patrons had no idea that she had been there. Now, in full view, with her violet eyes rivaling the

Cartier diamond for sheer beauty, she stood beside Burton and accepted the adoration.

"Thank you, thank you so much," she said, then added, "Shalom."

That did it. The audience cheered and applauded all over again, returning her greeting with shouts of "Shalom" and "Shalom Elisheba." She and Burton positively glowed. This was the attention that they had known for so long, the warmth from those who loved and appreciated them. It was intoxicating. It was addictive. And it was all theirs.

"The Biblical story of Ruth," Taylor began, "is about the first non-Jewish woman to convert to Judaism. It is a story of redemption and acceptance." As she spoke the sacred words, she turned to Burton and lifted her eyes to look into his. He returned her affection and immediately began speaking Shakespeare's most famous romantic sonnet, "Shall I Compare Thee to a Summer's Day," less to the audience that to her. It was not merely a theatrical moment, it was one that sprung from real life. When Taylor and Burton finished, their concentration was broken only by the extended applause.

I could see love in her face and I could see victory in his. With this achievement Richard Burton had reclaimed his self-respect not only as an actor but as a man.

After the performance, Taylor and Burton retired to the dressing room which was filled with dignitaries, many of whom had already opened the liquor bottles. When I found Burton in the crowd, he was holding a glass with a straw and lime slice. I stared at him and he left the people to whom he was speaking and stood within breath-smelling distance of me.

"Want a sip?" he asked. I looked at the drink. I hesitated. "Either you trust me by now, Yoram, or you never will." I changed the subject.

"You were amazing, Richard. It's an evening no one here shall ever forget, especially me." I shook his free hand. "Welcome back."

Jason approached Taylor. "If it's all right with you, Miss Taylor, I'll put the object back in safekeeping." Burton unfastened it from Taylor's neck and handed it to Jason.

I didn't expect Dieter to make an appearance after the screed that Burton had read to him over the letter, even though he seemed to warm to him at the Peres dinner. All things considered, I must compliment him on his bravery and tenacity: he showed up in the dressing room to pay his respects. Burton immediately saw him and walked briskly over. Dieter stiffened in anticipation, but Burton was all smiles.

"In the first flush of success, all is forgiven," Burton said. "Thank you for bringing us to Israel."

"You're welcome, Mr. Burton," Dieter said apprehensively.

"And I hope you get to make your film when the time is right."

"Yes," Dieter mumbled, not sure what Burton meant. "When the time is right."

"I assume you will want to direct," Burton added.

Dieter was even more stunned.

"Let me give you some advice," Burton offered. "First, learn how. *Auf wiedersehen.*"

"*Auf wiedersehen,*" Dieter said instinctively. Burton walked away.

By now Taylor had pulled Teddy Kollek away from the others and was charming him with all her powers. "Surely," she purred, "the Mayor of Jerusalem knows a rabbi who'll marry a Jewess and a shaygetz." She was trying to sound informal—*shaygetz* is Yiddish for a Gentile man—but she was desperately serious.

Kollek, as clever a man as he was a politician, didn't want to say "No" even when he couldn't say "Yes." "I'll see what I can do," he offered in an attempt to placate her. No fool either, this let her know that the marriage could not happen in Israel.

By this time, I was on the phone with Ani covering my other ear so I could hear her. She sounded excited but I couldn't make out what she was saying. "A what?" I said, "You'll have to speak up. It's noisy here. Yes, I'll be home soon. What's that?"

"It's a gift," I heard Ani say. "What I want to know is who sent it. It came anonymously." When I got home I saw what she meant: the appliance store had delivered a top-of-the-line washer-dryer to our upstairs apartment.

The next morning as Burton and Taylor departed from the King David Hotel for the airport, everybody came out to bid them farewell and tell them how much they enjoyed having them stay there: the hotel manager and his staff, and Ani, Dory, and me as well. A few photographers were still there to memorialize the moment, and the celebrity couple pretended to be irritated by them even as they played to their cameras. Burton helped Taylor into the back of their limo while a bellman packed the separate car with everyone's luggage.

"Thank you for the washer-dryer," Ani told the couple.

"I saw that you needed one," Taylor said. "It's my pleasure."

Before they rolled up the windows for privacy, Burton beckoned me over to take my hand. "Some day when you have a real movie to produce, think of me. Make it something worthy of your talent."

"And yours, too," I said.

"Of course," he smiled, "all this publicity has put my fee back where it belongs."

We shared a laugh. Suddenly I remembered something. I reached into my pocket and handed him paper money.

"What's this for?" he said.

"Give it to a needy person when you land. It's an old Jewish tradition. If you are traveling on a goodwill mission, God will protect you."

Taylor heard us. "Does it work on film critics?"

Burton and I let it pass. "Good bye, my friend," he said. "Be well. And, give my regards to, um, 'The People of Israel.'"

With that final quote, he rolled up the window and they drove off.

Unable to remarry in Israel because of the difference in their religions, Burton and Taylor managed to retie the knot two months later—October 10, 1975—in, of all places, Botswana, Africa. The setting was the Chobe Game Preserve with reporters kept far away thanks to a strong metal fence and the presence of wild lions. Under a makeshift chuppah erected outside the bungalow office of the game warden, Taylor and Burton were married by the District Commissioner of the nearby town of Kasane. Two locals served as witnesses, and the game warden's wife produced a glass at the appropriate moment for Burton to step on and break, as Jewish tradition dictates.

"Mazel tov," everyone said.

Taylor and Burton kissed, then Burton took a small Instamatic camera from his pocket and handed it to the game warden's wife.

"Would you mind?" he asked.

"I don't know how to take pictures," she said, "I'm not a professional."

"I know, I know," he assured her. "It's not for publication. It's just for the two of us."

The game warden's wife obliged and snapped a picture. When they got back to Switzerland, Burton sent it to the pharmacy for processing.

A week later, the "private" photograph made the front page of every tabloid in the world. The headline read, "Liz & Dick Re-Marry." To this day I don't know whether the leak was planned or not.

Yes I do.

And the speed with which it appeared in supermarket checkout lines everywhere was proof that Elizabeth Taylor and Richard Burton were again back on top.

Epilogue

IT WAS A PRIVILEGE TO be so close to Elizabeth Taylor and Richard Burton, whom I admired, even if it was only for a few days. I feel honored to have seen them in a way the public never saw them: as people. I never in my life dreamed that I would be so close to anybody as famous as they were. It's different now. Modern actors seem obsessed with being just like average people (except when it comes to salaries). In those days, a star was a star. Men patterned themselves after the way actors acted and what they said. Women would go to the movies just to see what the stars were wearing on the screen. Today people still go to the movies, but not for the costumes; instead, they watch what the female stars wear on the red carpet at the Oscars.

Burton and Taylor were among the last of a breed. Today with the Internet and YouTube and social media it seems that anybody can be a star, but when everybody is a star, then nobody is.

Taylor and Burton never appeared in another film together. They divorced again ten months later on July 29, 1976.

In 1977 Burton made a triumphant return to the Broadway stage in Peter Shaffer's play *Equus* playing a psychiatrist who tries to determine why a young man has blinded six horses in a fit of religious fervor. The play, which was loosely based on an actual incident in England, had opened on October 24, 1974 with another Welshman, Anthony Hopkins, as the doctor. In 1976 Anthony Perkins took over the role and, when he gave notice, the producers contacted Burton to see if he wanted to step in. This would be Burton's first stage experience since his evening of readings at the Jerusalem Theatre and, more importantly, the first time in a decade he would interact with other performers on the boards, as opposed to film. As an experiment, he substituted for Perkins on one memorable matinee.

"I've never been so bloody scared in my whole life," he told *The New York Times*'s Mel Gussow.[1] "I was trembling." When the Stage Manager announced, "At this performance, the part of Martin Dysart will not be played by Tony Perkins," the audience gave a groan of disappointment. But when he continued, "The part of Martin Dysart will be played by Richard Burton," the entire house stood up and cheered.

Burton played Dysart for twelve exciting, sold-out weeks. At the next Tony Awards, he was given a special "Welcome back to Broadway" statuette. But even that wasn't enough to restore his screen stardom. When the film of *Equus* was announced, the producers wouldn't consider Burton and insisted on going after Hopkins. To prove that he could still carry a picture, Burton took the role of Father Philip Lamont in *The Heretic: Exorcist II* (1977), the hotly anticipated sequel to *The Exorcist* (1973). *The Heretic* crashed and burned but, before it did, Burton was indeed given the lead in the filmed *Equus* (1977), which also performed poorly, but not before earning Burton his seventh and final Oscar nomination. He returned to Broadway in 1980 for a revival of his 1960 hit *Camelot* and again in 1983 for a limited run in Noël Coward's comedy *Private Lives* in which he co-starred with Elizabeth Taylor. By that time the couple had been divorced for nearly seven years. During the run, Burton married Sally Hay. Taylor was again single.

Richard Burton died of an intracerebral hemorrhage in Geneva, Switzerland, on August 5, 1984 at the age of 58. He was never cited for honors by the Queen of England, perhaps because he fled the UK for a tax haven in Switzerland.

Elizabeth Taylor devoted much of her time and energy in her later years to raising awareness of AIDS for which she was celebrated the world over. In 2000 she was made a Dame of the British Empire by Queen Elizabeth II. Although she married twice more—to Senator John Warner (December 4, 1975 to November 5, 1982) and Larry Fortensky (October 6, 1991 to October 31, 1996)—friends say that she never stopped loving Burton—and the State of Israel. She made several more trips there from 1976 on and showed her support of the country in numerous ways, from co-narrating the Holocaust documentary *Genocide* (1981) to signing letters protesting the U.S.S.R.'s treatment of Soviet Jewry, to offering herself in exchange for the 108 hostages being held by Palestinian and German terrorists at Entebbe airport in 1976.

In 1978, after the divorce from Burton, she sold the Cartier Diamond to Harry Lambert for $5 million (that's $18.9 million in today's dollars).

---

1. February 27, 1976

According to one report, she insisted that apart of the sale money would help finance a hospital in Botswana, Africa.

Taylor died in Los Angeles on March 23, 2011 of congestive heart failure at the age of 79.

For the longest time I wondered why Burton even considered, much less accepted, taking the role in our film. Certainly he didn't need the $50,000—not after dropping $1,050,000 for the Cartier diamond six years earlier as a present to Taylor. I also weighed conversations I have had in the years since his visit with those who were swept up in the madness, and feel confident in these recreations of his and Taylor's private conversations—if not the exact words, then surely the emotions behind them.

But did he visit Israel only for the publicity of re-marrying Taylor? A man as worldly as Burton should have known that a mixed religious marriage was impossible under Israeli rabbinical law. Or did he actually sense that he could redeem himself and rekindle his spirit in the land that had nurtured so many faiths? Alas, he chose never to write about it or discuss the matter. In the time I spent with him, much of it just the two of us, I sensed that he drew courage and renewal from treading the same earth as the Prophets. It happens to many Jews who visit Israel, so why not a Presbyterian from Wales? It also doubtlessly came from his charity performance at the Jerusalem Theatre, an event so powerful that, all these years later, those of us who were there continue to remark on it. The film and the publicity were just a byproduct.

Dieter Kraus continued to try to get his project off the ground for years to come but never did. Presumably, the rights to *Vergeltung* are still available.

I became an international film producer and made motion pictures with the major studios in Hollywood.

Not bad for someone who is in the business of air.

Appendix

THE AUGUST 30, 1975 PROGRAM for Richard Burton's appearance at the Jerusalem Theatre is not available, nor is a recording of the presentation. This Appendix contains selections of Biblical and classic literature that he drew upon during his and Elizabeth Taylor's memorable performance.

The Twenty-Third Psalm (English)
The Lord is my shepherd; I shall not want.
He makes me lie down in green pastures.
He leads me beside still waters.
He restores my soul.
He leads me in paths of righteousness for his name's sake.
Even though I walk through the valley of the shadow of death,
I will fear no evil, for you are with me.
Your rod and your staff, they comfort me.
You prepare a table before me in the presence of my enemies;
You anoint my head with oil; my cup overflows.
Surely goodness and mercy shall follow me all the days of my life,
And I shall dwell in the house of the Lord forever.

The Twenty-Third Psalm (Welsh)
Yr Arglwydd yw fy bugail; Ni fyddaf eisiau.
Mae hi'n fy ngwneud i orwedd mewn porfeydd gwyrdd: mae'n fy arwain at y dyfroedd llonydd. porfeydd glaswellt tendr: Heb. dyfroedd tawelwch
 Mae'n adfer fy enaid: mae'n fy arwain yn llwybrau cyfiawnder er mwyn ei enw.

Yea, er fy mod yn cerdded trwy ddyffryn cysgod y farwolaeth, ni ofnaf dim drwg; canys ti gyda mi; dy wialen a'ch staff maen nhw'n fy nghysuro.
Yr ydych yn paratoi tabl ger fy mron ym mhresenoldeb fy ngelynion: ti'n eneinio fy mhen ag olew; Mae fy nghwpan yn mynd yn rhy fawr. Heb. gwneud braster
Yn wir bydd daioni a thrugaredd yn fy nghefn i gyd holl ddyddiau fy mywyd: a byddaf yn preswylio yn nhŷ'r Arglwydd byth byth. hyd hyd y dyddiau

A Psalm of David (phonetic Hebrew)
Echsar lo roee Adonai L'David mizmor. Yarbitzeini deshe binot
Y'nahaleini menuchot al-me V'maglei yancheini y'shovei nafshi
Sh'mo l'man tzedek
Tzalmavet b'gei ki-eileich gam
Emadi ki-ata ro eira lo
Y'nachamuni hema u'mishantecha shivtecha
Tzor'rai neged shulchan'fanai taatockh
R'vaya kosi roshi v'shemen dishanta
Yird'funi va'chesed tov ach
V'shavti chayyai kol-y'mei
Yamim l'orech Adonai b'beit

The Song of Solomon
The beauty of Israel is slain on your high places.
How the mighty have fallen!
Tell it not in Gath,
Proclaim it not in the streets of Ashkelon-
Lest the daughters of the Philistines rejoice.
Lest the daughters of the uncircumcised triumph.
O mountains of Gilboa,
Let there be no dew nor rain upon you,
Nor fields of offerings.
For the shield of the mighty is cast away there!
The shield of Saul, not anointed with oil,
From the blood of the slain,
From the fat of the mighty,
The bow of Jonathan did not turn back,
And the sword of Saul did not return empty.

Saul and Jonathan were beloved and pleasant in their lives.
And in their death they were not divided;
They were swifter than eagles,
They were stronger than lions.
O daughters of Israel, weep over Saul;
Who clothed you in scarlet, with luxury;
Who put ornaments of gold on your apparel
How the mighty have fallen in the midst of the battle!
Jonathan was slain in your high places.
I am distressed for you, my brother Jonathan;
You have been very pleasant to me;
Your love to me was wonderful,
Surpassing the love of women.
How the mighty have fallen,
And the weapons of war perished!

Henry V (St. Crispin's Day speech)
What's he that wishes so?
My cousin Westmoreland? No, my fair cousin:
If we are mark'd to die, we are enough
To do our country loss; and if to live,
The fewer men, the greater share of honor.
God's will! I pray thee, wish not one man more.
Rather proclaim it, Westmoreland, through my host,
That he which hath no stomach to this fight,
Let him depart; his passport shall be made
And crowns for convoy put into his purse:
We would not die in that man's company
That fears his fellowship to die with us.
This day is called the feast of Crispian:
He that outlives this day, and comes safe home,
Will stand a tip-toe when the day is named,
And rouse him at the name of Crispian.
He that shall live this day, and see old age,
Will yearly on the vigil feast his neighbors,
And say 'To-morrow is Saint Crispian"
Then will he strip his sleeve and show his scars.
And say 'These wounds I had on Crispin's day.'
Old men forget: yet all shall be forgot,

But he'll remember with advantages
What feats he did that day: then shall our names.
Familiar in his mouth as household words
Harry the king, Bedford and Exeter,
Warwick and Talbot, Salisbury and Gloucester,
Be in their flowing cups freshly remember'd.
This story shall the good man teach his son;
And Crispin Crispian shall ne'er go by,
From this day to the ending of the world,
But we in it shall be remember'd;
We few, we happy few, we band of brothers;
For he to-day that sheds his blood with me
Shall be my brother; be he ne'er so vile,
This day shall gentle his condition:
And gentlemen in England now a-bed
Shall think themselves accursed they were not here,
And hold their manhoods cheap whiles any speaks
That fought with us upon Saint Crispin's day.

Richard II (**Hollow Crown speech**)
No matter where; of comfort no man speak:
Let's talk of graves, of worms, and epitaphs;
Make dust our paper and with rainy eyes
Write sorrow on the bosom of the earth,
Let's choose executors and talk of wills:
And yet not so, for what can we bequeath
Save our deposed bodies to the ground?
Our lands, our lives and all are Bolingbroke's,
And nothing can we call our own but death
And that small model of the barren earth
Which serves as paste and cover to our bones.
For God's sake, let us sit upon the ground
And tell sad stories of the death of kings;
How some have been deposed; some slain in war,
Some haunted by the ghosts they have deposed;
Some poison'd by their wives: some sleeping kill'd;
All murder'd: for within the hollow crown
That rounds the mortal temples of a king
Keeps Death his court and there the antic sits,

Scoffing his state and grinning at his pomp,
Allowing him a breath, a little scene,
To monarchize, be fear'd and kill with looks,
Infusing him with self and vain conceit,
As if this flesh which walls about our life,
Were brass impregnable, and humor'd thus
Comes at the last and with a little pin
Bores through his castle wall, and farewell king!
Cover your heads and mock not flesh and blood
With solemn reverence: throw away respect,
Tradition, form and ceremonious duty,
For you have but mistook me all this while:
I live with bread like you, feel want,
Taste grief, need friends: subjected thus,
How can you say to me, I am a king?

Hamlet **(Hecuba speech)**
Now I am alone.
Oh, what a rogue and peasant slave am I!
Is it not monstrous that this player here,
But in a fiction, in a dream of passion,
Could force his soul so to his own conceit
That from her working all his visage wanned,
Tears in his eyes, distraction in his aspect,
A broken voice, and his whole function suiting
With forms to his conceit? And all for nothing.
For Hecuba!
For what is Hecuba to him or he to Hecuba
That he should weep for her? What would he do
Had he the motive and the cue for passion
That I have? He would drown the stage with tears
And cleave the general ear with horrid speech,
Make mad the guilty and appall the free,
Confound the ignorant, and amaze indeed
The very faculties of eyes and ears.
Yet I, a dull and muddy mettled rascal, peak
Like John-a-dreams, unpregnant of my cause,
And can say nothing; no, not for a king,
Upon whose property and most dear life

A damned defeat was made.
Am I a coward?
Who calls me "villain?" Breaks my pate across?
Plucks off my beard and blows it in my face?
Tweaks me by the nose? Gives me the lie i' t' throat
As deep as to the lungs? Who does me this? Ha!
'Swounds, I should take it, for it cannot be
But I am pigeon-livered and lack gall
To make oppression bitter, or ere this
I should have fatted all the region kites
With this slave's offal.
Bloody, bawdy villain!
Remorseless, treacherous, lecherous, kindless villain!
O vengeance!
Why, what an ass am I! This is most brave,
That I, the son of a dear father murdered,
Prompted to my revenge by heaven and hell,
Must, like a whore, unpack my heart with words
And fall a-cursing like a very drab,
A scullion! Fie upon't, foh!
About, my brain. Hum, I have heard
That guilty creatures sitting at a play
Have, by the very cunning of the scene,
Been struck so to the soul that presently
They have proclaimed their malefactions.
For murder, though it have no tongue, will speak
With most miraculous organ. I'll have these players
Play something like the murder of my father
Before mine uncle. I'll observe his looks.
I'll tent him to the quick. If he do blench,
I know my course. The spirit that I have seen
May be the devil, and the devil hath power
T' assume a pleasing shape. Yea, and perhaps
Out of my weakness and my melancholy,
As he is very potent with such spirits,
Abuses me to damn me. I'll have grounds
More relative than this. The play's the thing
Wherein I'll catch the conscience of the king.

Under Milk Wood
To begin at the beginning:
It is spring, moonless night in the small town, starless and bible black, the cobblestreets silent and the hunched, courters and rabbits' wood limping invisible down to the sloeblack, slow, black, crowblack, fishingboatbobbing sea. The houses are blind as moles (though moles see fine tonight in the snouting, velvet dingles) or blind as Captain Cat there in the muffled middle by the pump and the town clock, the shops in mourning, the Welfare Hall in widows' weeds. And all the people of the lulled and dumbfound town are sleeping now.
Hush, the babies are sleeping, the farmers, the fishers, the tradesmen and pensioners, cobbler, schoolteacher, postman and publican, the undertaker and the fancy woman, drunkard, dressmaker, preacher, policeman, the webfoot cocklewomen and the tidy wives. Young girls lie bedded soft or glide in their dreams, with rings and trousseaux, bridesmaided by glowworms down the aisles of the organplaying wood. The boys are dreaming wicked or of the bucking ranches of the night and the jollyrodgered sea. And the anthracite statues of the horses sleep in the fields, and the cows in the byres, and the dogs in the wetnosed yards; and the cats nap in the slant corners or lope sly, streaking and needling, on the one cloud of the roofs.
You can hear the dew falling, and the hushed town breathing. Only your eyes are unclosed to see the black and folded town fast, and slow, asleep. And you alone can hear the invisible starfall, the darkest before dawn minutely dew-grazed stir of the black, dab-filled sea where the Arethusa, the Curlew and the Skylark, Zanzibar, Rhiannon, the Rover, the Cormorant, and the Star of Wales tilt and ride.
Listen. It is night moving in the streets, the processional salt slow musical wind in Coronation Street and Cockle Row, it is the grass growing on Llaregyb Hill, dewfall, starfall, the sleep of birds in Milk Wood.

The Song of Ruth
Entreat me not to leave you,
Or to turn back from following after you;
For wherever you go, I will go;
And wherever you lodge, I will lodge;
Your people shall be my people,
And your God, my God
Where you die, I will die
And there will I be buried.
The Lord do so to me, and more Also,
If anything but death parts you and me.

Sonnet 18
Shall I compare thee to a summer's day?
Thou art more lovely and more temperate:
Rough winds do shake the darling buds of May,
And summer's lease hath all too short a date;
Sometime too hot the eye of heaven shines,
And often is his gold complexion dimm'd;
And every fair from fair sometime declines,
By chance or nature's changing course untrimm'd;
But thy eternal summer shall not fade,
Nor lose possession of that fair thou ow'st;
Nor shall death brag thou wander'st in his shade,
When in eternal lines to time thou grow'st:
So long as men can breathe or eyes can see,
So long lives this, and this gives life to thee.

About the Authors

YORAM BEN-AMI has worked with major studios and networks. He is the first Israeli producer to have an American film open as the number one box office attraction: *Lone Wolf McQuade*, starring Chuck Norris, David Carradine, and Barbara Carrera, directed by Steve Carver. Ben-Ami and Carver optioned the rights to the script for $1 and it became a phenomenon spawning the long-running TV series *Walker, Texas Ranger*. He is an active member during Oscar season of the Academy of Motion Picture Arts and Sciences, and is a member of the Directors Guild of America and the Producers Guild of America. He lives in Los Angeles.

NAT SEGALOFF is a producer, teacher, and film historian who began his career as a studio publicist. He has written over a dozen books including biographies of Arthur Penn, William Friedkin, and Harlan Ellison. For BearManor Media he has written *Final Cuts: The Last Films of 50 Great Directors; Screen Saver: Private Stories of Public Hollywood; Screen Saver Too: Hollywood Strikes Back; Stirling Silliphant: The Fingers of God*, and *Mr. Huston/Mr. North: Life, Death, and Making John Huston's Last Film*. He lives in Los Angeles.

Acknowledgments

Photographs that initially appeared in *Ma'ariv* newspaper are used through the courtesy of, and with permission of, the Government Press Office of Israel, Ilana Dayan, Office Director. The author expresses thanks to her as well as to Nat Segaloff; Ben Ohmart of Bear Manor Media; Jane Shalom of The Jerusalem Foundation; Dory Ben-Ami, Steve Carver, Lori Cohen, Rudy Cohen, Kevin Connor, Gavin de Becker, Ziggy Gilboa, Yoni Hamenachem, Susan Jaffee, Margot Klausner, Amos Mokadi, Udi Nedivi, Mace Neufeld, Zev Radovan, and Netta Shadmi.

> Yodo Productions, Ltd.
> 19528 Ventura Boulevard
> P.O. Box 182
> Tarzana CA 91356

Index

A

Absalom 64
Africa 126, 129
Albee, Edward 73
Al-Hasad, Hafez 108
alcohol 20, 53, 100, 106
anti-Semitism 58
Arabs 41, 58, 66, 100, 116
Armenia 64
Ashkenaz 120
Assyrian 40
Attenborough, Richard 10

B

Babylonians 64
Barbarians 100
Bar-Lev, Haim 88
Becket 62
Ben-Ami, Ani (ne; Nedivi) v, 2, 3,
    9-12, 23-25, 37-38, 51-52,
    84, 90, 91, 97-98, 106, 117.
    141 Photos: 73, 83
Ben-Ami, Dory 45, 46, 91, 97, 98,
    105-107, 114, 125, 141
Ben-Ami, Yoram's father 11, 12, 98
Ben-Ami, Clara (mother) 3, 4
Ben-Ami, Yoram (also Yoram, Benny)
    3, 4, 10, 11, 13, 23, 27-28,
    31, 34-35, 39-42, 46, 49, 54,
    59, 6-, 67, 72, 74, 77-78, 91,
    94, 96, 99, 109, 110, 115,
    124, 139
Ben-Canaan, Ari 11
Ben-Gurion 42, 46, 63, 115

Blacklist 9
bodyguard 42, 48, 59, 61, 67, 68, 75, 80
Bonnecarrère, Paul and Joan
    Hemingway 10
Botswana, Africa 126, 129
Broadway 48, 117, 120, 127, 128
Burton, Richard (also Dick) 3, 4, 7,
    9-11, 13, 15-25, 29-43, 45, 46-
    69, 71-77, 79-84, 87-91, 93-
    101-103, 105-111, 113-117,
    119-129, 131, 133-135, 137
Burton, Sybil (ne: Williams) 16, 119
Butterfield-8 74

C

Camelot 120, 128
Carradine, David 82, 139
Carrera, Barbara 139
Cartier (necklace) 16, 59, 61, 80, 120,
    124, 128, 129
Carver, Steve 82, 139, 141
Christians 63, 64
Churchill, Winston 17, 18, 79
chutzpah 10, 31, 42, 111
circumcision 45, 105, 106, 114
Cleopatra 16, 39, 49, 53, 65, 74, 119
Clinton, Bill 12
Coburn, James 19
Coleridge, Samuel Taylor 48
Comedians, The 16
Connor. Kevin 141
Cottle, Graham 10, 11
Coward, Noel 128

D
David (king) 122
Dayan, Moshe 107
De Becker, Gavin 141
DeMille, Cecil B. 40
diamond (Cartier) 16, 56, 59, 61, 63, 75, 80, 120, 124, 128, 129
divorces (various) 9, 16, 23, 24-25, 57, 73, 115, 127-128
Dysart, Martin 128

E
Egypt 42, 51, 63
Elisheba (Taylor's Hebrew name) 51, 58, 68, 124
England (Britain, London) 7, 10, 17-19, 48, 62, 118, 122, 117, 127, 128, 134
Entebbe 128
Equus 127, 128
Exodus 9-11, 19, 31, 40
Exorcist, The 128

F
Fellini, Federico 94
Fink, Ilan 33-35
Fisher, Eddie 16, 48, 57
Flynn, Errol 12
Fortensky, Larry 128

G
Geneva, Switzerland 30, 36, 38, 128
Gilboa, Ziggy 80, 132, 141
Goldbogen, Avram (Mike Todd) 57
Goldstein, Nathan 35, 38, 67
Gorman, Cliff 10
Gussow, Mel 128

H
Hadassah 24
Hamenachem, Yoni 91, 81, 141
Hamlet 117, 123
Hashem 66, 106
Ha'aritz 94
Hay, Sally 120
Hebrew 19, 58, 78, 95, 115, 117, 121, 132

Heifetz, Yascha 12
Hemingway, Joan 10
Heretic, The 128
Hollywood 9, 12, 15, 27, 30, 37, 55, 57, 62, 63, 74, 79, 91, 108, 117, 129, 139
Holocaust 57, 128
Hudson, Rock 22
Huppert, Isabelle 10
Huston, John 139

I
Internet 15, 127
Isaac (son of Abraham) 106
Israel 7, 9-12, 16, 17, 19, 21, 22, 24, 25, 27, 28, 31-36, 39, 41, 42, 47-50, 52, 53, 56-58, 63, 66, 67, 74, 77, 78, 80, 81, 83, 84, 86-88, 90, 91, 93, 96, 97, 99, 100, 107, 110, 111, 113, 115-117, 119, 120, 122-126, 128, 129, 132, 133, 139, 141

J
Jaffa 64, 99
Jenkins, Richard (Burton) 119
Jerusalem 39-41, 52, 59, 60, 63-66, 75, 80, 82, 86, 89, 90, 93, 94, 96, 99, 100, 102, 110, 113, 115, 117, 119, 120, 125, 127, 129, 131, 141
Jesus 19, 64, 71
Jewison, Norman 19
Jews 12, 24, 48, 57, 63, 64, 67, 73, 99, 100, 105, 109, 120, 126, 128, 129
Joyce James 48
Judaism 48, 51, 65, 66, 86, 105, 124

K
Kasane Game Preserve 126
Katrina 28, 38
Keats, John 48
kibbutz 60
Kiddush 115

Kissinger, Henry 40-42, 47-51, 55, 59-63, 68, 69, 75, 80, 82, 87, 90, 93, 108, 116
Kissinger, Nancy 47, 49, 51, 61, 67-69, 80, 87, 90, 96
Klotzky, Maurice 30, 36, 38
Koch, Ed 63, 86
Kollek, Teddy 39, 59, 63-69, 75, 80, 86, 90, 101, 102, 120, 121, 125
kosher 106
Kraus, Dieter 9, 21, 27-33, 38-40, 42-43, 45-50, 54-58, 64-65, 67-69, 71, 75, 88, 94-98, 105-116, 124, 125, 129

L
Lambert, Harry 128
Lancaster, Burt 12
Laura 9
Lone Wolf McQuade 82, 139
Luftgeschäft ("the business of air") 12

M
Masada 78, 94-96
Ma'ariv 83, 84, 87, 88, 141
Mitchum, Robert 10, 19
Muslim 63, 64, 99

N
Nadler, Michael 65
Newman, Paul 11
Nicholson, Jack 12
Norris, Chuck 82, 139
Nussbaum, Max (rabbi) 57

O
Oscars (Academy Awards) 4, 12, 15, 74, 122, 127, 128, 139
Ottomans 99
O'Neal, Tatum 23
O'Toole, Peter 10, 117

P
Palestine 12, 128
paparazzi 15, 56, 87, 94
Peck, Gregory 4

Peres. Shimon and/or Sonia 89, 113-117, 124
Perkins, Anthony 127, 128
Phoenician 40
Polish 107
Pontrhydyfen, Wales 101, 119
Porgy and Bess 9
Preminger, Otto 9-11, 19, 31, 33, 40, 81, 114
Presbyterian 129
Press, reporters, paparazzi 7, 9, 13, 16, 24, 33, 40, 41, 42, 47-52, 54-58, 63, 67, 68, 73, 75, 76, 83, 84, 87, 88, 90, 94, 101, 126, 141

R
Rampling, Charlotte 19
Romans 66, 78, 86, 99, 100
Rosebud 10, 11, 19, 81
royalty (description) 3, 4, 9, 10, 12, 16, 18, 20, 22, 24, 28, 30, 32, 34, 36-38, 40, 42, 46, 48, 50, 52-54, 56, 58, 60, 62, 64, 66, 68, 72, 74, 76, 78, 80, 82, 84, 86, 88, 90, 94, 96, 98, 100, 102, 106, 108, 110, 112, 114, 116, 119, 120, 122, 124, 126, 128, 132, 134, 136, 138
Ruth 124, 138

S
sabbath 89, 102, 110, 113, 115, 116, 119
Samuel 64, 121
sandek 106
Sandpiper, The 16
Saul 122, 132, 133
Schmidt, Gunter 75, 96-98, 107
Shadmi, Netta 4, 141
Shakespeare 25, 48, 58, 73, 111, 117, 122, 124
Sherover, Miles 65
Silliphant, Stirling 139
Sisco, Joseph 41, 43, 49-51
Solomon 64, 100, 101, 111, 132

T

tabloids (supermarket) 15, 16, 23, 37, 38, 76, 102, 126
Taming of the Shrew, The 16, 25
Taylor, Elizabeth (also Liz) 3, 4, 7, 9, 11, 13, 15-17, 19-25, 29, 31, 33, 35, 37-39, 41-43, 46-69, 71-77, 79-84, 87-91, 93-97, 99-103, 105-111, 113-117, 119-129, 131, 133, 135, 137
Taylor-Burton 42, 80
Tel-Aviv 17, 72, 97
Thomas, Dylan 48, 117, 123
Tisch, Edwin John (Eddie Fisher) 58
tracheotomy (Taylor's) 74
Trumbo, Dalton 9

U

Uris, Leon 9

V

Vergeltung (script) 13, 19-21, 22, 25, 27-29, 30, 33, 37, 38, 47, 48, 50, 53, 55, 57, 65, 74, 75, 88, 91, 96, 97, 101, 108, 129, 139

W

Wales, Welsh 21, 22, 24, 73, 80, 99, 100, 119, 121, 123, 127, 129, 131, 137
Walker, Texas Ranger 82, 139
Wayne, John 12

Y

Yoram (see Ben-Ami, Yoram)

Z

Zanzibar 137
Zurich, Switzerland 24, 47

www.ingramcontent.com/pod-product-compliance
Lightning Source LLC
Chambersburg PA
CBHW070811100426
42742CB00012B/2333